9/06

Woodbridge Town Library
Woodbridge, CT 06525

A2180 181562 4

Livin' La Vida Low-Carb

My Journey From Flabby Fat To Sensationally Skinny In One Year

DUE

D1113960

Copyright © 2005 Jimmy Moore

10-Digit ISBN 1-59113-804-3
13-Digit ISBN 978-1-59113-804-4

All rights reserved. No part of this publication may be reproduced, stored in a retrieval system, or transmitted in any form or by any means, electronic, mechanical, recording or otherwise, without the prior written permission of the author.

Printed in the United States of America.

Contact the author at livinlowcarbman@charter.net or http://livinlavidalocarb.blogspot.com/

Livin' La Vida Low-Carb

My Journey From Flabby Fat To Sensationally Skinny In One Year

Jimmy Moore

Important Medical Disclaimer
for <u>Livin' La Vida Low-Carb</u>

JIMMY MOORE IS PROVIDING <u>LIVIN' LA VIDA LOW-CARB</u> (HEREAFTER REFERRED TO AS "BOOK") AND ITS CONTENTS ON AN "AS IS" BASIS AND MAKES NO REPRESENTATIONS OR WARRANTIES OF ANY KIND WITH RESPECT TO THIS BOOK OR ITS CONTENTS. JIMMY MOORE DISCLAIMS ALL SUCH REPRESENTATIONS AND WARRANTIES, INCLUDING FOR EXAMPLE WARRANTIES OF MERCHANTABILITY AND FITNESS FOR A PARTICULAR PURPOSE. IN ADDITION, JIMMY MOORE DOES NOT REPRESENT OR WARRANT THAT THE INFORMATION ACCESSIBLE VIA THIS BOOK IS ACCURATE, COMPLETE OR CURRENT.

The statements made about products and services have not been evaluated by the U.S. Food and Drug Administration. They are not intended to diagnose, treat, cure, or prevent any condition or disease. Please consult with your own physician or healthcare specialist regarding the suggestions and recommendations made in this book.

Except as specifically stated in this book, neither Jimmy Moore nor any authors, contributors, or other representatives will be liable for damages arising out of or in connection with the use of this book. This is a comprehensive limitation of liability that applies to all damages of any kind, including (without limitation) compensatory; direct, indirect or consequential damages; loss of data, income or profit; loss of or damage to property and claims of third parties.

This book provides content related to topics about weight loss, nutrition and health. As such, use of this book implies your acceptance of the terms described herein.

You understand that a private citizen without any professional training in the medical, health, or nutritional field authored this content. You understand that this book is provided to you without a health examination and without prior discussion of your health condition. You understand that in no way will this book provide medical advice and that no medical advice is contained within this book or the content provided.

You understand that this book is not intended as a substitute for consultation with a licensed healthcare practitioner, such as your physician. Before you begin any weight loss program, or change your lifestyle in any way, you will consult your physician or other licensed healthcare practitioner to ensure that you are in good health and that the examples contained in this book will not harm you.

If you experience any unusual symptoms after following any information from this book, you will immediately consult with your healthcare practitioner.

You understand that the information and content of this book should not be used to diagnose a health problem or disease, or to determine any health-related treatment program, including weight loss, diet, or exercise.

You understand that there are risks associated with engaging in any activity described in this book. Any action you take implies that you assume all risks, known and unknown, inherent to lifestyle changes, including nutrition, exercise and any other physical activities and/or injuries which may result from the actions you take.

You hereby release Jimmy Moore and the publisher from any liability related to this book to the fullest extent permitted by law. This includes any damages, costs, or losses of any nature arising from the use of this book and the information provided by this book, including direct, consequential, special, punitive, or incidental damages, even if Jimmy Moore have been advised of the possibility of such damages.

Your use of this book confirms your agreement to the above terms and conditions. If you do not agree, you will not utilize this book and will request your full refund within the timeframe specified in your contract of sale.

Acknowledgments

Writing a book is definitely not a one-man show as most people might think. It takes a concerted effort on the part of some patient individuals to make something like this come together for you the reader to enjoy.

While the writing process itself and the thoughts embodied in this book came solely from me and my experience losing 180 pounds on a low-carb lifestyle in 2004, I certainly could not have accomplished such an enormous feat as writing my first book without the help of some very special people all along the way.

First, let me thank God for placing within me a passion and desire for writing and telling others about the incredible health benefits of low-carb as evidenced by my own transformational weight loss success story. His guiding Hand over my life over these past two years especially has enabled me to accomplish more than I could have ever imagined and I am eternally grateful for the blessings He has given me. To God be the glory and praise for what He has done and continues to do through my life.

Second, one of those blessings from the Lord is my beautiful and lovely wife, Christine. She played such an integral role throughout the entire process of losing the weight and writing this book, including providing me with inspiration for losing weight, encouragement to stay on the program when things got difficult, and loving me every step of the way. She also was one of my most faithful proofreaders and literally rewrote the entire book from start to finish for me as I was going through the final manuscript edits. Christine, you are the sunshine and joy of my life and I hope the rest of our lives will be just as exciting as the first ten years have been together! I love you more than you'll ever know! Be sure to read her comments about what it was like "Livin' With The Low-Carb Man" at the end of this book.

Third, my other proofreaders Mary Boan and Cathy Lancaster were so faithful and dedicated to provide me with constructive feedback about my book as well as catch those tiny little typographical mistakes that I missed along the way. You ladies are true gems and I will forever be grateful for your assistance with this project. Thank you so very much!

Fourth, I am very appreciative to Ralph Bristol for his unique role in my weight loss story. Ralph is a local radio talk show host in Greenville, South Carolina and had an interesting part in my weight loss story that you will read about in the Introduction. He was even gracious enough to agree to write the foreword to this book and I am confident you will enjoy what he has to say about me and my weight loss journey. Ralph is a gifted writer and communicator and I am deeply indebted to him for taking time out of his extremely busy schedule to help me out in this endeavor.

Fifth, I want to recognize all of my low-carb friends who have supported me at my successful "Livin' La Vida Low-Carb" blog (livinlavidalocarb.blogspot.com). The enormous outpouring of appreciation and steadfast support from people like Jonny, Carla, Linda, Adam, Regina, Katherine, Duncan, Levi, Kalyn, and so many more others I have met and could keep naming has shown me that this low-carb community is built around a solid group of people who are sincerely dedicated to this healthy lifestyle choice for the rest of their lives and want others to experience what it has to offer them as well. That's my goal with this book, too, and I hope to carry the torch high enough to make each of these newfound friends of mine proud.

Sixth, the book you are reading right now would not have been possible without the enormous foresight and vision of a company called Booklocker.com. They were willing to step up to the plate and allow this former 410-pounder tell my story about how I went from flabby fat boy to the fabulously fit man I am today.

Booklocker.com's innovative spirit regarding books and authors will surely make them one of the most influential independent book companies of the 21st Century! I hope I can make them as proud of <u>Livin' La Vida Low-Carb</u> as I am!

Seventh, I am honored to have had my manuscript reviewed by Jacqueline A. Eberstein, R.N., the co-author of <u>Atkins Diabetes Revolution,</u> who worked with Dr. Robert Atkins for nearly three decades in all aspects of his organization. Using her expertise in nutrition as the director of nutrition information for Atkins Health & Medical Information Services, Jacqueline was gracious enough to offer a few suggestions to help me make this book the best it could be. I am grateful for her insight and professional review of my book and for her very insightful quote for the back of the book.

Finally, let me say one more big thank you to YOU. Whether you are overweight or have a friend or loved one who needs to find some way to lose some excess pounds, thank you for deciding to get this book about my weight loss experience. It was the single biggest accomplishment of my life and I hope it gives people the inspiration and determination within themselves to finally do it this time and keep it off for the rest of their lives. Isn't that what we want so we can stop the endless cycle of failed diets?! Absolutely.

If you commit yourself right now to be proactive in tackling your weight problem, then I am here to tell you that nothing can stand in your way of being just as successful as I was. It's not going to be easy at first, but it's not impossible and you will survive, I promise. Let my story show you that your dream of losing weight and keeping it off can and will become a reality for you, too!

Contents

Foreword by Ralph Bristol

If you want to lose weight, you need more than just advice. You need inspiration. If losing weight didn't involve a degree of hard work, sacrifice and commitment, the word "obesity" wouldn't even be in the dictionary. No one wants to be fat. Americans are fat because we instinctively indulge ourselves, and we don't have the inspiration to change.

To do the healthy thing, we need not just instruction, but inspiration. In <u>Livin' La Vida Low-Carb</u>, Jimmy Moore dishes out healthy portions of both.

Moore is not a doctor or a professional dietitian. He learned how to lose weight the low-carb way like a dogged investigative reporter and self-appointed guinea pig all rolled into one. A plainspoken man, Moore tells it like it is in language that anyone can understand.

He discovered that living a healthy low-carb lifestyle is itself a form of indulgence. It brings him much more pleasure and satisfaction than the indulgences to which he was previously attached.

In the process, Moore transformed himself from a 410-pound mass of sweaty fat to 230 pounds of energy and muscle. When you do that – and enjoy it as much as Moore has – it's hard to keep the story to yourself.

Go ahead. Indulge yourself – the "Livin' La Vida Low-Carb" way.

Ralph Bristol is a radio talk show personality and host of "The Ralph Bristol Show" on Newsradio 1330/950 WORD-AM in Greenville/Spartanburg, SC, www.ralphbristol.com

Introduction

The latest statistics from the U.S. Centers For Disease Control and Prevention reveal that nearly two out of every three Americans are either overweight or obese and that number is still on the rise in virtually every state. That is a haunting statistic that every man, woman, doctor, politician, and health expert in this nation should be concerned with as we look to the future. It is obvious to me that whatever we are currently doing is not working and something desperately needs to be done to help people deal with the growing problem of obesity.

But what can people do to lose weight and keep it off for good when there are so many seemingly conflicting messages about what is good for your health and what is not? How do you know which diet plan is going to help you find that elusive permanent way to lasting weight loss?

I had to personally come to terms with those questions myself in early 2004 and decided for myself that I would try livin' la vida low-carb. That's the catchy little phrase I like to use to refer to the decision I made to start eating an entirely different way from what I was used to eating. This experience has so radically transformed my life that I just had to write a book to tell the whole world about it.

The seemingly impossible task of writing a book like this one about my weight loss experience was indeed a daunting one that I had to contemplate in many hours of thought and prayer. While I am used to writing short essays on a variety of subjects on the Internet, I have never written an entire book before and it was indeed a challenge like none other I have ever gone through in my entire life. But, looking back on it now, if I was able to find it within me to lose 180 pounds in about a year, then writing a book should be a piece of cake (as long as it's low-carb, of course!).

This book was a labor of love birthed out of the tremendous outpouring of support I have received from friends, family and even complete strangers who told me they were motivated and inspired by my weight loss success story. After I lost my weight, so many people would come up to me asking my advice about what I did to lose weight so it could possibly help them in their own weight loss efforts. After telling my story at least a hundred or so times, several people suggested that I write a book. So here it is.

It has been an unbelievably incredible journey for me to travel down and I am extremely humbled to have been able to accomplish this feat thanks to the strength God gave me throughout the entire process to make it happen. And I give Him all the glory for this because without Him, I could do nothing. Both the weight loss and this book have shown me in a dramatic way that with God all things really are possible for anyone who dreams big.

What you are about to read in the upcoming pages of this book is my own personal account of how I successfully lost a lot of weight and have kept it off permanently. I would caution you about trying to exactly replicate everything that I did to lose weight while livin' la vida low-carb because everyone's body is different. While what I did worked for me, that doesn't necessarily mean it will all work for you in the same manner. But I hope my story can at the very least inspire you to lose weight if that is something that you need to do.

In case you are wondering, I am not an expert on the subject of weight loss and health by any stretch of the imagination nor do I claim to have all the answers to your specific weight situation. If you have any questions about your health, then I highly recommend you consult your doctor since he has been trained to deal with such issues. I am just one man sharing my story of successful and permanent weight loss.

Also, if you are wanting to know more about the actual process of low-carb and why it works, there are plenty of books out there that can give you the scientific data and history about low-carb and what it is about. If you are unsure about which low-carb program you might be interested in trying, then I highly suggest you pick up Jonny Bowden's <u>Living The Low-Carb Life</u> which gives an overview of all the low-carb plans out there and helps you decide which one will work best for you. The purpose of my book is to simply share with you my anecdotal experience of what I did to lose weight and sharing with you the lessons I learned following a low-carb lifestyle.

As I look back on my life that began anew on January 1, 2004, I will always remember that specific date as a significant life-changing mile-marker that forever altered my future. It was on that fateful day that I was bound and determined to not only make losing weight my New Year's resolution that year, but also to make it my New Life resolution to keep it off once I lost it! Although I had tried many diets in my life, succeeded at losing weight on many of them, and predictably failed to keep it off (and actually gaining back an additional 25 pounds or so each time, too!), somehow this time was going to be different. Little did I know just how incredibly different it would actually be.

I can remember that embarrassing day that I went to weigh myself on a special industrial-sized scale for heavy cargo so I could get my starting weight for my "diet" (I will explain later why I don't like to use the term "diet" regarding my weight loss). It's funny now, but I weighed way too much for conventional scales which cannot register weights more than 300 pounds. I knew I weighed a whole lot more than 300, but how much more?

As if being on a scale like that wasn't embarrassing enough, staring with utter disbelief at those three big red digits on this gigantic scale like a deer in headlights absolutely startled me to the core. 4-1-0!!! Did that scale really read four-hundred and ten pounds?!?!! Are you kidding me?! How in the world did I ever allow myself to get that big?! Aaaaackkk! Needless to say, I was quite disturbed.

After the initial shock of discovering what I weighed began to wane, I quickly realized that 410 pounds was my reality. I knew I was a big man at 6'3" tall, wearing size 62/32 pants and 5XL shirts, but 410 pounds was absolutely enormous. I know it's going to be hard for some people to believe, but I never even realized I had actually gotten that big until I was already there.

Most of us don't have the luxury of seeing ourselves as others see us every day unless you vainly stare at the mirror for hours on end. But it really would do us all a lot of good if we would take some time to look at our bodies and determine if the physical condition we are in is where we need to be. For many of us, we have a lot of work to do.

That's exactly where I was physically in January 2004. I had allowed myself to become this behemoth monster of a man, but now I was bound and determined to lose weight and never ever get that heavy again. This epiphany is the breakthrough moment that anyone who ever hopes to lose weight for good needs to go through. You will not be able to deal with your weight problem as long as you refuse to acknowledge that you have one in the first place.

Unfortunately, a lot of people probably think that people who are overweight and obese already know they are that way and just refuse to do anything about it. While I agree that there are some overweight and obese people who have completely given up on trying to lose weight and just don't care anymore because of their repeated failures on various diet programs, the overwhelming majority of overweight and obese people would undoubtedly say we would like to do something about our weight problem if we could just find that key method or solution to make it happen for us. For far too long, nothing we have tried seems to work. We are on the brink of throwing in the towel on trying to lose weight because it seems like a hopeless cause. Believe me, that is exactly where I was for most of my life.

Pick a diet, any diet and I bet you I have done it at one point or another.

Powder diets. Rabbit food diets. 1500-calorie-a-day diets. Starve yourself diets. Any and every diet you have ever heard of, dream up, or fooled me into thinking might work I had tried. And many of them produced marginal success until I got off the "diet" itself. The vicious cycle of "lose, gain, lose, gain some more" seemed like a perpetual problem I would have to deal with for the rest of my life.

My first glimpse of tremendous success on a weight loss plan was when I actually lost an astounding 170 pounds in 1999 following a low-fat diet and had gotten skinnier than I had ever been in my entire adult life up until that point. But, guess what happened? Within a year of losing that enormous amount of weight, I had ballooned back up to my previous weight and then some. That scenario had pretty much been my life's story up until the first day of 2004. By the grace of God, though, from that day forward I would never be the same again!

I had already heard about the Atkins diet from some friends who had some modest weight loss success on it themselves. I can vividly remember hearing them talk about the foods they were eating and all I could think about was just how crazy they must be stuffing their faces with all of that fat.

We have become so conditioned by low-fat advocates and even our own government standards that boldly declare fat is bad for you and that eating low-fat is considered healthy that my initial gut reaction to Atkins was to avoid it like the plague. I was so indoctrinated with the low-fat lie that I didn't even want to give this weight loss method a real chance to work for me.

I remember when I lost all of that weight in 1999, many people just automatically assumed that I had done it on Atkins since I lost as much as I did. I can remember angrily responding, "No way, are you kidding me? I wouldn't be caught dead doing that diet because it's not safe." I was such a dope at the time. Little did I know that just five short years later I would be doing the very same diet I was condemning so harshly and would become one of its strongest advocates.

Prior to starting the Atkins plan in 2004, I had not properly educated myself on what all it entailed. I just assumed it was a diet that let you eat all the meat, cheese and eggs you wanted without any consequences. If you ask most people about low-carb, that's probably how most of them would describe it, too. But I had not studied for myself the tremendous health benefits of a low-carb lifestyle and was completely ignorant of how and why it worked.

That's why in December 2003 I decided to buy the bestselling book by the late Dr. Robert Atkins, the father of the low-carb eating lifestyle that began in the early 1970s, called Atkins New Diet Revolution. This book goes into great detail about what all is involved in doing the Atkins version of the low-carb lifestyle, including what foods can be eaten, the four distinct phases of the plan, weight loss success stories, recipes and more. For anyone who is serious about doing Atkins by the book, then this is the absolute first step to doing it the right way.

Don't fall into the trap that I did of assuming you know what Atkins is and how to do it. Just get the book and read about it for yourself. With more than 45 million copies sold worldwide, a lot of people are intrigued by success stories they hear from people like me. That was one of the deciding factors in my decision to write this book because there were so many people asking me to share my story to help them, a friend or a family member with their weight problem.

While many so-called health "experts" have issued warning after warning about the alleged dangers of doing a low-carb lifestyle, real-life examples like myself have proven that these alarmists are simply ignoring the fact that this way of eating really works for people. Their "the-sky-is-falling" warnings are just their opinions based on what they were taught in medical school which was based on the mistaken notion that a portion-controlled, low-fat, and low-calorie diet is the only effective way to lose and maintain your weight.

Yet, the fact that the low-fat diet is a very heavily-promoted, but failed weight loss approach combined with the truth that these negative claims against low-carb have not been substantiated by any long-term medical research tell me it is a bit premature to totally dismiss this weight loss solution as a viable option for people who are overweight or obese. I'll talk about how I personally became carb-conscious on my way to livin' la vida low carb in Chapter 1.

But, as you will quickly notice as you navigate through this book, I am going to be completely honest with you about my own experiences on the low-carb lifestyle. Let me tell you, those first few days on Atkins were really, really hard for me. Actually, the first day I thought I was literally going to die, I'm not kidding you. Ask my wife, she'll tell you how utterly miserable I felt. I even called my local talk radio station on New Year's Day 2004 while the host was discussing weight loss resolutions and I shared how awful I felt being on the first day of my Atkins diet.

My body ached like it has never ached before and I had the worst possible pounding headache I had ever had in my entire life. With all of this going on in my body, I could barely move. I have no doubt in my mind that my body was going into shock from my soda withdrawal, which I had been used to drinking nearly 200 ounces per day! Yes, I said 200 ounces per day, equivalent to over one and a half cases of 12 ounce cans per day. I'll talk about this subject in greater detail in a later chapter, but all you need to know is that this was the most difficult physical challenge I had ever gone through. Thankfully, though, it didn't last.

The good news is that it only got better from there physically as the pain from the first day quickly began to subside. Within a week, I had replaced drinking all those sugar-filled sodas with caffeine-free diet sodas as well as guzzling nearly 2 gallons of water per day. That certainly made for an interesting period of my life when I got to know the inside of the men's restroom very well. But it was a necessary change that made an incredible difference once the weight started pouring off. The impact that water can have when you are livin' la vida low-carb is the subject of Chapter 2.

Did I mention the weight started pouring off of my body immediately and in bunches? In my first week alone, I lost an eye-popping 15 pounds! I was totally stunned by this weight loss total and it showed me this low-carb thing was really working! Although I expected it to work, I had no idea it was going to work this well this fast! I became even more convinced of how effective it was when I lost another 8 pounds in the second week and a grand total of 28 pounds in the first month alone. Woo hoo! I was definitely loving livin' la vida low-carb, baby!

Around the end of January 2004, a local radio talk show host from WORD 1330/950AM in the Greenville/Spartanburg, SC area named Ralph Bristol, who wrote the foreword to this book, started talking about conducting a weight loss contest on his afternoon show. He wanted to feature people who were dangerously obese and hoped to create an incentive to help them lose weight. When I heard this, I thought to myself, "Yeah, that's me! I could do that!" The name of the weight loss contest was "Ralph's Incredible Shrinking Ton" and it was to feature five contestants who cumulatively weighed a ton, or 2000 pounds.

I enthusiastically contacted Ralph via e-mail as he requested and told him how much I weighed as part of the process of becoming part of the contest. I was hopeful I would be chosen as one of the five, but I didn't know if my weight was going to be heavy enough for the contest since he was looking for five people who each averaged 400 pounds. Since I had already lost nearly 30 pounds on my low-carb program before I heard about this contest, I knew I was hovering around 380 pounds when I entered myself as a possible contestant.

Ralph responded back to me that although my body mass index was lower than any of the other four contestants, he would still like for me to be one of his five "Incredible Shrinking Ton" participants to compete for an array of prizes from local sponsors. The contest was scheduled to run from the last Friday in January through the Friday before Thanksgiving in a race to see who could lose the most weight as a percentage of their starting weight over that time period.

Since I had already lost nearly 30 pounds on Atkins before this contest began, I was ostensibly at a slight disadvantage from the start. But I was certainly not worried about that because I knew I had a whole lot more weight to lose.

On the day of the weigh-in at the radio station, I stepped up on that big digital scale and was pleased to confirm my weight loss progress up to that point. But I was still a very big boy weighing in at a hefty 382 1/2 pounds and had plenty of fat to lose for the duration of the contest.

My competitors in the contest included two other men and two women and we were all extremely big people. In fact, one of the guys in the contest named D.R. weighed in at a staggering 619 pounds! He was doing Atkins like me and had the ability to lose a lot of weight, too. Because of that, I knew I had my work cut out for me to compete with D.R. in this contest. But I was determined to win that contest.

With a weight loss contest on the radio to help keep me accountable, I decided for the first time in my life to exercise. Oh, yes, that dreaded word for so many of us lifelong couch potatoes who shudder at the very mention of the word. For 32 years of my life on earth, I had never even cared to participate in any organized daily exercise plan. But now I was about to embark on an exercise routine for the first time ever because I knew it would be essential to my success at losing weight.

Beginning with the treadmill and gradually working my way up to the elliptical and Stairmaster machines, this aspect of my weight loss plan was extremely challenging, yet rewarding. In Chapter 3, I will discuss about how beginning an exercise routine was such an integral part of my weight loss success and how I almost quit exercising altogether during an especially difficult period.

With this new way of eating well underway and daily exercise incorporated into my weight loss efforts, I knew I needed to add some supplemental vitamins to help me keep my energy level up and to provide my body with the nutrients it needed to function at optimum level. I started off with a multi-vitamin, but eventually progressed to adding fish oil, fiber, calcium and even potassium (you'll find out later why this nutrient is extremely important to add to your diet when you are on a low-carb lifestyle!). Read about the crucial role these and other vitamins played in my weight loss success in Chapter 4.

Well, I got through the month of February and quickly dropped another 40 pounds that month, which took my total weight loss to nearly 70 pounds in just the first two months. Holy cow, this is the best diet program I've ever seen in my entire life! Am I ever livin' la vida low-carb!

A lot of people want to know what motivated me to get started on a low-carb lifestyle to begin with. That's difficult to say because it wasn't just one thing, but rather a series of events that led me to begin this exciting way of eating and losing weight. I hope you enjoy reading my responses to a list of the top ten arguments people have against the low-carb lifestyle. It will arm you with clear facts to counter the ways people will try to discourage you as you begin this way of eating for yourself. This chapter is a must-read because you will encounter a lot of misinformation from uneducated people when you are on a low-carb program and you will need to be motivated to stick with it despite their negativity. I will share with you what motivated me to finally begin livin' la vida low-carb in Chapter 5.

I will readily admit that one of my biggest weaknesses prior to beginning Atkins was sugar. Can I get a witness anyone?! Whether it was cookies, cakes, candy bars, cheesecake, or chocolate chip cookie dough ice cream, I loved and craved anything and everything that had lots and lots of sugar in it. I could never get enough of it (and that was evident by the enormous belly that was protruding out the front of my body!) because I was literally addicted to it as so many people who are overweight or obese are.

But all that had to change forever when I started livin' la vida low-carb because sugar is the most basic form of carbohydrate there is. UGH! The fact is though sugar is arguably more responsible for the obesity problem that so many of us face in this country than the much more demonized fat. I'll explain this in greater detail and share with you how I kicked the sugar habit for good in Chapter 6.

If I have heard it once, then I've heard it a million times. "Atkins is just too boring. You have to eat the same foods over and over again and it's just not worth the trouble." While some people on a low-carb lifestyle may choose the same low-carb foods to enjoy over and over again, most successful people on this kind of eating plan have learned to add some variety to their plate with great-tasting recipes borne out of a little creativity with those foods considered "legal" when you are livin' la vida low-carb. Getting creative when you are eating low-carb foods is the subject of Chapter 7.

While God is undoubtedly the centerpiece of my life and He guides my every step, I am extremely thankful for my wife, Christine, who has been and will always be my most influential motivation on this earth. But I would be completely remiss to not recognize others like Rodney at my local YMCA and Harlan from my church who faithfully stood by my side throughout this experience and gave me the exact words of encouragement when I needed them the most. I'll talk about the importance of having a strong support system of friends, family and even complete strangers in Chapter 8.

I was absolutely loving my new eating lifestyle and the results it was producing during those first few months on Atkins. But soon my elation would turn to concern when I hit my first weight loss stall. This was the true test of my willingness to keep going even when the going got tough.

By April, my total weight loss had reached a mind-boggling 85 pounds and I was riding high on the thrill of weight loss nirvana. I was even talking about the prospect of reaching my weight loss goals much sooner than I would have ever expected and did not envision anything that would get in the way of that.

But then it happened. Sccccccrrrrrrreeeeeecch! BAM! What happened?

You guessed it! That was the horrifying sound of my weight loss coming to a complete and utter standstill. The scale just refused to go down even a pound or two for the first time since I had started Atkins. Not just one week, two weeks, or even a month. For the next 10 weeks in a row (yes, two and a half months!), I did not lose a single pound, not a one.

At first, it really didn't bother me much because I had expected my weight to stall eventually and I had already done much better than I could have ever expected. But I certainly didn't expect the stall to last as long as it did. This is when the mental aspect of losing weight comes into play and unfortunately can derail the efforts of so many people who would otherwise do well in their weight loss had they just stuck with it just a little longer. Sound familiar?

Thankfully, though, my faith and inner determination kept me from so easily giving up on this worthy endeavor despite my bleak circumstances. It was my first real challenge of livin' la vida low-carb and it forced to me deal with reality face-to-face. Was I going to give up on it now despite my early success or would I allow it to be my catalyst for a renewed motivation to continue on? Obviously, based on my eventual success I chose the latter. But because many people have so easily given up at the first sign of difficulty in their weight loss, I will share with you ten ways that I was able to persevere in my weight loss to reach my goal weight and keep it off for good in Chapter 9.

Finally, in Chapter 10, I discuss the importance of transforming the "diet" aspect of low-carb into a real commitment to do it for the rest of your life. Too many other diets have failed to help people maintain their weight loss because they have not shown people how to permanently change their eating habits. They give you a temporary way to lose weight, but they don't show you how you can keep that weight off for good.

That is why I don't like using the term "diet" to describe livin' la vida low-carb. Eating this way is not just a temporary way to lose weight, but rather a lifelong journey to keep the weight off forever. Discover the lessons I learned about making this lifestyle change permanent as I share with you some of my experiences I have been through since losing all that weight.

So there you have it. Those are the ten life-changing characteristics that have helped me take off 180 pounds, dropping my total cholesterol to 140 from over 300 including raising my good cholesterol from 30 to 70, lowering my triglycerides from 200 to 50, watching my resting heart rate fall from 85 to 50, increasing my exercise from virtually none to 10-15 hours per week, going from a size 62 pant size to a size 40, shrinking my shirt size to a loose XL from a tight 5XL, and seeing many other areas of my health get significantly better as a result of livin' la vida low-carb.

By the way, remember the radio weight loss contest? I was the eventual winner, but there's a story behind it that's too funny not to share. It turns out that three of the other contestants decided to drop out of the contest long before the weigh-in date in November, which left me to face D.R., the 619-pound contestant who had lost significantly more than 100 pounds himself during the contest based on his periodic updates on the radio show. But, on the day of the weigh-in, he was hospitalized for a health-related issue and could not make it to the radio station for the weigh-in.

Therefore, technically, I won the weight loss contest by default because nobody else showed up. But most people believe I would have probably won the contest anyway since I had lost about a third of my overall body weight from the time the contest started. In order for D.R. to have beaten me, he would have had to lose well over 200 pounds during the contest period. While that was not impossible for him to do since he was such a big guy, it wasn't very likely. It was definitely an immensely fun experience for me and I am thankful for the opportunity I was given to participate. Thanks so much, Ralph! I don't know if I could have done this without your contest to keep me accountable.

As you begin reading in the following pages about the ten key points to my weight loss success, I want you to think about something for just a moment. Imagine the 180 pounds that I lost was a bunch of sacks of potatoes. Now that's a whole lot of spuds, isn't it?! For just a moment now, close your eyes and think about how much weight you need to lose. Go ahead, close your eyes and see them for yourself. Can you visualize those potatoes (no, not to eat them!)? That's your weight crying out to you and begging to come off of your body. The time has come for you to begin the process of livin' la vida low-carb.

You will have the same ability to lose weight as I did if you apply these simple principles that you are about to read to your own life. There is absolutely nothing standing in your way of losing 10, 25, 50, 100 or even 200 pounds and keeping it off forever if that is what you want and need to do. But now it's in your hands. If you've read this far into the book already, then you must be serious about finally doing it. So get out there and start livin' la vida low-carb today!

Chapter 1
Becoming Carb-Conscious

Now that you are pumped and primed to finally do the low-carb lifestyle for yourself, it's time to dive right in to this exciting new way of life and start enjoying the tremendous health benefits that are waiting for you as you embark on this adventurous new journey.

If you are ready to go and have already read the low-carb book you have chosen to help you start livin' la vida low-carb (if you still haven't made up your mind about which plan you want to do, then you really need to pick up Jonny Bowden's <u>Living the Low-Carb Life</u> to help you get started on low-carb the right way), then here are a few quick pointers that will help you begin your transformation into becoming carb-conscious right away.

- Get on the Induction phase of about 20g carbohydrates per day and stick with it for the first two weeks. You may scoff at having to keep your carb intake so low at first, but it will be so worth it for you. You must resist the urge to cheat even a little bit. Make sure you eat the exact foods you are allowed to eat and in the amounts you are allowed to eat them in this early part of the process so your body can transform itself into the lean, mean fat-burning machine it was meant to be. This is non-negotiable and must be done without argument in order for you to begin losing weight on low-carb. Contrary to popular belief, you don't cut out vegetables when you are livin' la vida low-carb. in fact, you can eat four cups of salad greens per day during the Induction phase. Yummy!

- When you go to the grocery store to purchase food, you can easily compute what is called "net carbs" by subtracting the dietary fiber and all sugar alcohols from the total carbohydrates. For example, if a sugar free chocolate bar has 24 total carbohydrates per serving with 2 grams of dietary fiber and 21 grams of a sugar alcohol (such as maltitol or lactitol), then that product is considered to have 1g net carb per serving. These are the only carbs you need to count when you are livin' la vida low-carb. Dietary fiber and sugar alcohols are still carbohydrates, but they have very little effect on your blood sugar and do not need to be counted towards your total carbohydrate intake when counting carbs in most people. This method of computing total net carbs will help you decide what foods are best for you to consume while you are on your low-carb lifestyle.

- Try not to weigh yourself too much in the beginning because that can discourage you from continuing on with the plan and may derail you before you even get the train moving forward. However, if weighing yourself often motivates you, then do it. I personally enjoyed the thrill of weighing myself often because I liked watching the scale move. But try to find one consistent time to weigh yourself (in the morning right after I get out of bed seems to be the best time for me) to get an accurate measurement of your progress. The fantastic thing about being on a low-carb program is the fact that the weight tends to melt off of your body extremely fast during the first month or so of being on it. If you're not already, then you need to get excited about what is to come for you in the next few months and visualize it even now. Remember those sacks of potatoes? You can do it!!!

- Whatever you do, don't ever give up. No matter how much it may hurt, no matter how run down you may feel mentally or physically, no matter what your subconscious tells you, just don't give up. Believe me when I say that the low-carb lifestyle only gets easier the longer you stay on it. I will talk about some of the things that helped me persevere through the difficult times in a later chapter, but I want you to know right now that the minor struggle you may face in the beginning is all worth it in the end. The benefits greatly outweigh the little aches and pains that it took to get you there.

- Continue to educate yourself about the low-carb lifestyle by reading low-carb magazines and purchasing any of the library of excellent low-carb books and cookbooks that are easily accessible in bookstores and on the Internet. The fact that you are reading this book right now shows that you are fully committed to educating yourself even more about the low-carb way of eating. With so many recipes and ideas out there, it'll take you years to try them all. In fact, I'll share with you a few of my own favorite recipes at the end of this chapter. Whatever you do, though, don't be afraid to try something new. You may be surprised to learn that you actually like cauliflower or broccoli with cheese sauce now. In fact, I have a friend named Kalyn who created a low-carb recipe blog called "Kalyn's Kitchen" (kalynskitchen.blogspot.com) to show people how incredibly delicious livin' la vida low-carb can be for them through simple-to-follow recipes. When you visit, be sure to tell Kalyn that I sent you!

I knew from the very beginning of my new low-carb lifestyle that I was going to absolutely love it. As an avid fan of both cheese as well as fresh cut deli meats, I could not believe that both of these scrumptious foods were considered "legal" as part of a carb-conscious eating plan. Not only are they acceptable, but they are even encouraged! Livin' la vida low-carb never tasted so good, baby!

You may have already noticed that I call what I did to lose weight a "lifestyle," "program," "plan," or "way of eating" rather than a "diet." That is deliberate. It may just be semantics to some people, but when I think of a "diet" the first thing that pops into my mind are negative thoughts of food deprivation and a temporary way of eating until your weight loss goals are achieved so you can get back to eating "normal" again. Been there, done that, gained it back, no thanks! What is "normal" eating anyway? Does anyone really know?

When you choose to follow the low-carb lifestyle, that defeated mentality of being on a "diet" radically changes because you get to eat many great-tasting foods that can and will satisfy your hunger. Even more exciting than that is the fact that this low-carb way of eating will also become the way you will maintain your weight for the rest of your life long after the "diet" part of it is over. This is why people who eat a low-carb lifestyle not only lose a lot of weight, but can keep it off better than those who eat a low-fat diet. That is why this mindset of becoming carb-conscious in your eating habits is so vital to attaining the success you deserve while following a low-carb plan.

Nevertheless, there have been some naysayers who describe the selection of foods available on a low-carb program as too restrictive. It is clearly obvious to anyone who has educated themselves about this way of eating that there is a vast buffet of mouth-watering foods available to eat when you are livin' la vida low-carb. To be honest with you, my experience has shown me that following a low-fat diet is much more restrictive then a low-carb lifestyle and the foods on low-fat diets are not nearly as tasty and fulfilling as the low-carb foods are. There is just no comparison!

All you need to do is take just one bite of any low-fat cheese or meat to taste the clear difference between low-fat and low-carb. Eating low-carb foods has taught me that you can eat foods that taste good even when you are trying to lose weight and not feel guilty about it at all. On a low-fat diet, you simply don't have that option.

You will recall from the Introduction that I told you about my 170-pound weight loss on a low-fat diet in 1999. What I quickly discovered with a low-fat diet is that you can only keep up that way of eating for so long before you go absolutely nutty! Who could ever eat that way day in and day out for the rest of their life? Not me, that's for sure!

That was my undoubtedly my single biggest downfall on a low-fat diet. I simply could not keep it up over the long haul. It was so mundane and I felt like I was depriving myself of so many of the foods that I loved (and I was!). The food selection on my low-fat diet was severely limited and not nearly as desirable as the low-carb foods that I eat now.

You will find that when you are livin' la vida low-carb, the foods are much more interesting than any low-fat diet you've ever tried. What's not to like about eating foods such as eggs, cheese, chicken, hamburger, sausage, turkey, pepperoni, steak, salad, cream cheese, ham, strawberries, blueberries, low-carb breads and wraps, hot dogs, peanuts, almonds, macadamia nuts, green beans, low-carb peanut butter, real butter, Ranch dressing, pork rinds, real cream, real mayonnaise, sugar-free chocolates and much, much more? These are just a few of the hundreds of excellent foods I was able to consume when I started my low-carb lifestyle. It was the absolute best selection of foods that I had ever eaten on a weight loss program in my entire life! That sure made it a lot easier to stick with it throughout my weight loss and even now that I am maintaining my weight.

Just in case you are wondering, I do not miss pasta, bread or sugar at all. While I used to enjoy eating these and other carb-loaded foods like there was no tomorrow, I now know that they are not a part of a healthy eating lifestyle for me anymore. Besides, with so many tasty low-carb versions of virtually all of these foods available, if I get a craving for them then I can have them. My friend Linda owns an online low-carb food store based in Ohio where you can purchase zero-carb breads, snacks and more (www.kickthecarbz.com). You will be amazed by all the foods that are available to help you on your low-carb lifestyle.

While the low-carb versions of these foods are great, something interesting will begin to happen the longer you stay on your low-carb lifestyle. You will actually start to lose your desire to eat high-carb foods altogether. I know it may be hard to believe, but it's true! Even those foods that you thought you could never live without will begin to lose their appeal to you when you are livin' la vida low-carb. You don't believe me? Check out what happened to my desire for a particular food just months after I went on my low-carb program.

One of my favorite foods growing up and throughout most of my entire life has been macaroni & cheese. You can ask my wife or my mom and they will tell you that I could eat a whole plate of the stuff and go back for seconds (and thirds and fourths and...!) before I started on my low-carb lifestyle! In fact, my wife always joked with me that macaroni & cheese was it's own food group.

But now even the sight of macaroni & cheese literally disgusts me. I think it looks gross and all I can think about when I see it are all those carbs it contains! My mom thinks this is a sign of the impending apocalypse that her son doesn't like macaroni & cheese anymore! Yet these are the kind of unexpected changes that begin to happen when you start livin' la vida low-carb.

I have heard more than my fair share of people describe the low-carb lifestyle simply as the "meat diet" or the "bacon and eggs diet" with no restrictions on fat, meat or protein, but it is so much more than that. While it is true that you can eat those foods and still lose weight while following a low-carb program, the goal of an effective plan for losing weight and keeping it off is to find the low-carb foods that satisfy both your hunger and your taste buds. If you don't like any of the foods you are eating, then you won't be able to stay on the plan. Again, this was one of the major reasons why all those low-fat diets continued to fail me time and time again. I could not force myself to eat that way for the rest of my life.

It amazes me how the opponents of the low-carb lifestyle focus their attention so heavily on the fat content in the foods on a low-carb plan. "With all that fat, there's just no way that can be healthy for you," they smugly proclaim. Sadly, too many people actually believe that is the truth and blindly reject low-carb as a passing fad that cannot possibly be good for you. We have become so conditioned in this country to get uptight about consuming any fat because that message has been hammered down our throats for the past three decades. The government standards for diet and nutrition are supposedly infallible while we continue to ignore the clear evidence in study after study that has shown eating a low-carb lifestyle is a healthy alternative to restricting your fat intake for weight loss.

In fact, it is the fat and protein in the foods that you consume that keep you satisfied longer while you are on a low-carb lifestyle. While you are cutting your carbohydrate intake, your body is using the fat and protein in the foods you eat to make you feel full much longer than you would on a low-fat diet. This is a revolutionary concept that simply does not make sense until you educate yourself about the benefits of following this proven process.

Even more startling is what a May 2005 Washington University at St. Louis study found regarding the role of fat in weight loss. According to the research, people who severely restricted their fat intake were actually causing fat to store on their stomach, thighs and buttocks. The study also found that people who attempt to lose weight by severely restricting their fat intake will actually cause their weight to gain because their liver needs additional new fat to burn the stored fat in these areas of their body. Finally, researchers in the study said that consuming more dietary fat can be an effective means for burning fat and losing weight in those areas where low-fat has not worked.

Have you heard about this study before now? Probably not because it is not a message that low-fat advocates want you to hear. But this research basically confims that eating fat is a g-ggood thing. Wake up America, this is revolutionary! After years and years of being told we need to completely cut out nearly every gram of fat from our diets, now we're being told that probably wasn't the best advice for trying to lose weight. Unbelievable! Gee, what a surprise. You know, there might be hope yet for solving the obesity problem in this country if the whole truth about low-carb would start being told.

There are some people who incorrectly assume that the fats people consume on a low-carb lifestyle are mostly saturated fats. This is simply not accurate. Most of the fats that you put in your body when you are following a low-carb program are the good ones that your body needs to function properly and to help you lose weight.

For example, nuts are loaded with a high amount of the good fats that are prohibited when you are on a low-fat diet. But it can be argued that nuts are an important part of any healthy eating plan. Unfortunately for low-fat dieters, they are forced to avoid these nutritious and delicious foods altogether.

I received an e-mail from a woman who read an article I had written on the Internet about this topic that made me laugh because she was so worried that she was "cheating" and "doing bad" on her low-carb plan because of all the fat she was consuming. She was overcome with feelings of guilt because she had convinced herself that eating all that fat was so "unhealthy." Ugh!

My response to her was that she needed to permanently shake the fat-phobia mentality if for no other reason than to help her keep her sanity while doing a low-carb program. I assured her that eating fat was indeed a good thing when you are livin' la vida low-carb and not to worry about counting any fat grams or calories and you don't even have to worry about the portion size either. GASP! All of these things are unnecessary when you are on a low-carb lifestyle.

Make sure you read this next sentence very carefully to learn an important lesson as you are becoming carb-conscious. Whatever you do, don't try to mix both low-carb and low-fat in the same eating plan. It will only lead you to greater frustration and failure than any other weight loss plan you have ever attempted because you will be so hungry all the time and will prohibit low-carb from working the way it was designed to work. Low-fat and low-carb are as incompatible as oil and water.

You may be surprised to learn that most low-fat foods are actually higher in carbohydrates than their regular versions. When I visited my family last Christmas after being on a low-carb lifestyle for nearly a year and losing most of my weight, my thoughful sister Beverly had bought me a bottle of Ranch dressing at the grocery store since I told her it was an acceptable salad dressing for me to eat. However, when I looked at the bottle she had purchased for me, I noticed she got the fat-free version thinking it was supposed to be "healthier." Upon examining the label of this fat-free Ranch dressing, though, I noticed there were 6g carbs per serving. Interestingly, that exact same product has only 1g carb per serving in the regular full-fat version. This puts a whole new twist on what is considered "healthy" now, doesn't it?

The dirty little secret that low-fat food manufacturers won't tell you is that they have to flood their products with excessive sugar and salt when they remove the fat just to make them taste somewhat recognizable to their great-tasting regular versions. You will read in a later chapter about why consuming these extra hidden sugars is not good for you, especially when you are on a low-carb lifestyle. Suffice it to say that these little extras can cause more harm than good when you are attempting to lose weight and keep it off.

This is an important lesson as you learn to become carb-conscious. Don't assume that you know how many carbohydrates are in a food product you are buying, even the so-called low-carb foods on supermarket shelves today.

I made this mistake when I first started my low-carb plan and it caused me to buy something I would not have otherwise purchased had I been paying attention to the carb content. The specific item I got was a package of hot dogs. Since I had purchased hot dogs on a previous visit to the grocery store that only had 1g carb for each hot dog, I just assumed that all hot dogs had the exact same amount of carbohydrates. This was not very smart on my part!

That package of weiners I bought had an unbelievable 8g carbs for just one hot dog! I could not believe all the sugar and other additives that were in this product that would cause there to be such a wide discrepancy in the number of carbohydrates found in them. I learned an invaluable lesson right away that you need to read each and every nutritional label of every food product you intend to purchase to avoid falling into the trap of thinking you know the carb totals of a particular food. By the way, I ended up throwing away that entire package of hot dogs because 8g carbs for a single hot dog was just way to much for me! Good riddance!

I look back shamefully now on my strong criticism of the low-carb lifestyle in 1999 when I harshly scorned it for not making sense. The only reason it did not make sense to me at the time is because I did not allow myself to discover how and why the wonderful process of low-carb works. I had no idea at the time that eating a low-carb lifestyle could have benefitted me so much even as I was struggling to stay committed to my low-fat diet. While I regret gaining back all of that weight I had lost on the low-fat diet in 1999, I am certainly glad I found the low-carb pathway to a better and more permanent way of losing weight in 2004.

If you want a comprehensive explanation of how following a low-carb way of eating makes you lose weight, then you can read all about it in your favorite low-carb book (if you are still undecided about which one you want to do, let me remind you about <u>Living the Low-Carb Life</u> by Jonny Bowden which explains the science of low-carb in great detail).

In a nutshell, restricting your carbohydrate intake makes your body emit ketones during a natural process known as ketosis, which is your body's natural fat-burning method. It can take a few days for your body to enter ketosis as your body adjusts to consuming less carbs. Some experience ketosis in just a couple of days and for others it can take as much as a week. But getting your body into ketosis is how your body will begin losing weight on your low-carb program.

How do you know if you are in ketosis? I like to use ketone strips, available at your local pharmacy, to determine whether I am in ketosis or not. When ketosis is indicated on the test strip that only requires a small urine sample, then you will know that your body is burning stored fat. This is something you should be excited about as you are on your low-carb lifestyle. Being in ketosis is a very good thing.

But even if the test strips do not indicate that you are in ketosis, that does not mean you are not burning fat on your low-carb program. Some people may never see their test strips turn pink or purple, but will be losing weight and inches while livin' la vida low-carb. If the strips are continually showing no ketosis, then don't fret. You may be one of those lucky people who still lose weight without having excess ketones. Furthermore, when you start eating upwards of 40-50g carbs per day as you progress through the stages of your low-carb plan, ketone levels will be less and less. The bottom line is for you not to become discouraged if your test strips are not changing colors for you.

Keep in mind that the process of ketosis is a very safe way to lose weight and should not be confused with a similar sounding process diabetics have to be concerned with. Just remember that as long as you are in ketosis, your body will lose stored fat. Staying in ketosis is an invaluable key to successful weight loss on your low-carb plan.

It's a beautiful thing to see that ketone strip turn pink or purple when you check it every few days. The pure joy of knowing that you are doing something good to improve your overall health is what will drive you to continue on livin' la vida low-carb. It is something that will become a regular part of your life as you take the pounds off one-by-one until you reach your goal. The sweet thrill of triumph over your weight problem is so easily within your grasp.

But I must warn you of one slight side effect for people who are following a low-carb lifestyle. You may start to notice the smell of your breath and urine will change. One of the manifestations of higher ketone levels in your body is a strong odor in the breath and urine. This bothered me a little initially when I first started my low-carb program, but I quickly realized that this was simply an indicator that my body was burning a whole lot of stored fat. Over time the odor does begin to subside until you don't even notice it anymore. You should get extremely excited when the presence of ketones is strong because you know you are burning fat. If you are concerned that your breath stinks, then pop a sugar-free mint and you'll be good to go. Nothing is going to stand in your way of weight loss success this time! No excuses!

As you are becoming carb-conscious, keep in mind that food manufacturers won't always have the same definition of low-carb that you do. You simply cannot rely on a product that claims to be low-carb to be right for you. That is why reading labels is something you must do to lose weight on your low-carb lifestyle.

If you restrict yourself to about 20g net carbs in a day, then you are going to have to read labels very carefully and not just take the word of the box that blares the words "low-carb" on it. Unfortunately, food companies either don't understand what low-carb means or they just don't care. It appears that many of them are only interested in jumping on the low-carb bandwagon to sell products and make money. This is why so many of the low-carb products in the past year or so have failed because the food companies just don't get it. Even when Atkins Nutritionals, Inc. filed for bankruptcy protection in August 2005, it was because they were unable to properly gauge what people on a low-carb lifestyle actually wanted and were willing to spend money on. But the failure of these products doesn't mean people are no longer interested in this lifestyle. It simply indicates that consumers want better and less expensive products to eat on their low-carb program.

I can remember seeing a "low-carb" version of Hamburger Helper on the shelf when it came out in 2004 and could not believe it when I read that it contained an eye-popping 24g net carbs per serving. Wowsers! While this is probably "lower" in carbs than the regular Hamburger Helper, it certainly would not be described by me as a product that is "low-carb."

Then there's the highly-touted joke of a product called C-2 from Coca Cola. The marketing for this product bragged about how it has "half the carbs" of a regular Coke. While that statement is technically accurate, it still had 19g net carbs per serving. In a 20-ounce bottle of C-2 there are 2 1/2 servings, which amounts to a remarkable 48g grams of sugar carbs in this so-called low-carb Coke. No wonder Coke decided to pull the plug on this product in mid-2005 because low-carb consumers rejected the idea that this was a "low-carb" product as it was being marketed.

When you are limiting yourself to 20-40g carbs per day during the early phases of your low-carb lifestyle, consuming these kind of products can and will be extremely detrimental to your ultimate goal of losing weight. It is these kind of dishonest gimmicks from companies trying to take advantage of an uninformed public about low-carb that angers me to no end. Be cautious of any product claiming to be low-carb by reading the nutritional label for yourself to see if it passes the litmus test for being considered low-carb.

A poignant survey conducted by the popular eDiets.com web site in June 2005 found that one-fourth of Americans don't even know what a "carb" is and 60 percent of them have no idea what the low-carb lifestyle is all about. How are people supposed to make informed choices about how to lose and maintain their weight if they are not being given all the information they need to make such decisions? There's a lot of work left to be done to help educate the masses about the wonderful world of low-carb.

I have often been asked how many carbs I restricted myself to while I was losing weight. For me, I was comfortable eating 20g net carbs per day because that was the level of carb intake my body needed to lose weight during my weight loss phase. But that does not necessarily mean you will be on the same schedule. In fact, you may be able to eat a whole lot more carbs than I did. Everyone's body is different and you will have to find out for yourself the highest amount of carbs you can eat in a day and still be in ketosis.

Once you discover how many carbs you are allowed to consume each day, that is when the fun begins. It's time to eat! Woo hoo! I'm talking about the juiciest, most mouth-watering, scrumptious morsels of food that have ever touched your lips on a "diet." Okay, that may be just a bit hyperbolic, but compared to low-fat diets this really is heaven!

The most popular question people ask me about livin' la vida low-carb is about what foods I ate. That has always amused me somewhat because I don't have a set meal plan for each day. I just eat and keep track of my carbs. Even still, people have asked me to share with them some of the recipes I have concocted since starting my low-carb lifestyle that I have found to be both appetizing and delicious. The following are just a few of my favorite original low-carb recipes that I could literally eat over and over again until the good Lord calls me home:

BACON CHEDDAR RANCH CHICKEN MELT
Fry 2 frozen boneless, skinless chicken breasts in a skillet with real butter until it is thoroughly cooked and golden brown on the outside, add crumpled bacon and cheddar cheese on top until melted, move chicken breasts from the skillet to a plate and generously pour Hidden Valley Ranch dressing on top. Mmmm! This recipe will make you slap your momma silly (sorry mom!) and is an absolute winner that will keep you coming back for more. Containing just 6g net carbs for this entire meal, you could have it for lunch and dinner and still have plenty of carbs to spare!

NAKED BACON CHEESEBURGER
Fry 2 hamburger patties in a skillet until thoroughly cooked, add bacon and American cheese on top until melted, move burgers to a plate with large leaves of lettuce, and add real mayonnaise and mustard on the side. Who said you can't enjoy a bacon cheeseburger when you are livin' la vida low-carb?! The best part is this simple, yet fulfilling recipe contains only 2g net carbs. Can you see how keeping your carb intake around 20g in a day is not as hard as people are making it out to be?

PEPPERONI MELT
Take 2 low-carb wraps (be careful when you purchase these and make sure they have 5 net carbs or less for each wrap) and put your favorite cheese in the middle, distribute about 12-15 pepperoni slices on top of the cheese, fold the sides and roll like a burrito, and then microwave for about 45 seconds. Ooh la la,

this quick and easy meal has 12 net carbs and it is worth every last bite!

MASHED CAULIFLOWER
Boil a bag of frozen cauliflower until very tender, mash and then blend until creamy. Add real butter, your favorite cheese, sour cream and chives for a great alternative to mashed potatoes. You won't even realize you are eating cauliflower and will be pleasantly surprised how amazingly close to mashed potatoes this recipe actually tastes! At just 3g carbs per serving, you'll make this side dish a staple in your low-carb lifestyle. I bet your family won't be able to tell the difference between this and mashed potatoes!

CHOCOLATE PEANUT BUTTER CHEESECAKE BALLS
Mix one 8 oz. block of Philadelphia cream cheese, 2 tablespoons of Carb Options Skippy peanut butter, 1 teaspoon of vanilla and a cup of Splenda with an electric mixer until thoroughly blended (it will be extremely thick). Refrigerate for an hour until firm, shape into quarter-sized balls on a sheet of wax paper, roll balls in crushed almonds or peanuts until thoroughly covered, melt 2 Z-Carb bars (www.zcarb.com) in the microwave and generously drizzle on top of each ball and refrigerate for an hour before serving. These delectable dessert balls have only 2g net carbs each and will satisfy even the worst sweet tooth you'll get. This one is so good that it will shock your friends who may be skeptical of low-carb. Wait until you see the look on their face when you tell them it's low-carb!

STRAWBERRY CHOCOLATE CREAM PARFAIT
Slice a pound of fresh strawberries in a bowl, mix them with sugar-free strawberry gelatin until well blended, scoop into parfait glasses adding whipped cream after each scoop, and pour melted Z-Carb chocolate bars on top of the whipped cream for the best-tasting, most refreshing dessert you've ever had! This luxurious and satisfying treat contains only 6g net carbs.

It's an ongoing joke between myself and my wife when I complain to her tongue-in-cheek how much I'm "suffering on my diet" when I eat these and other low-carb recipes. Oh the spoils of livin' la vida low-carb!

Another common question I get from people is regarding going out to eat. More specifically, they ask me "what do you order when you go to a restaurant?" Most of the time I explain that many restaurants will be very accommodating to people on a low-carb lifestyle and will allow appropriate substitutions to make virtually any meal low-carb.

For example, Denny's has a menu item called the Meat Lover's Breakfast, which features eggs, sausage, ham, bacon, hashbrowns and pancakes. In lieu of the hashbrowns and pancakes, they allow me to have an extra egg or two as well as some cheese on top or even a side salad. This meal ends up totaling only about 4g net carbs and is great for anyone following a low-carb plan.

I also like going to Chick-Fil-A for their chargrilled chicken. Oh my goodness, nothing tastes better than a grilled-to-perfection golden brown chicken breast with a slice of American cheese and mayonnaise. This is yummy to my tummy with only a couple of carbs for the cheese. In fact, the employees at my local Chick-Fil-A are so used to me ordering this that they don't even ask what I want to order most of the time because they already know.

In addition, there are other restaurants that already cater to those of us on low-carb lifestyles such as Subway. Their low-carb wraps are incredibly tasty and filling. My favorite one is the Chicken Bacon Ranch wrap. At 12g net carbs, these are a great offering for people who want a quick and satisfying low-carb meal.

Then there is Hardee's which came out with the low-carb Thickburger and low-carb Breakfast Bowls in 2004. Both of these products show me that company has a genuine commitment to cater to those of us who are carb-conscious. I can appreciate any company who makes an effort to reach the low-carb community with menu items that are truly low-carb and not just in name only.

My experience on a low-carb lifestyle has been that most steakhouses allow their customers to substitute green beans or a salad for the potato and bread. Be sure to watch out for any carrots and croutons on your salad because they are loaded with carbohydrates. Also, choose your salad dressing carefully and ask for regular Ranch or vinegar and oil dressings to avoid the hidden sugars that are commonly found in most salad dressings.

You may have noticed that I haven't recommended that you purchase very many of the wide array of low-carb products on the supermarket shelves today. My low-carb friends affectionately call these products "Frankenfoods" because they are fake versions of foods you are not allowed to eat while on low-carb. Although some of these products are nice to have every once in a while, you will find that they will not be your primary foods when eating low-carb.

With that said, if you find something you like and can still lose weight when you eat it, then keep buying it. That's exactly what happened for me when I purchased Dreamfields brand of low-carb pasta. It was so good and yet I still lost weight while using it that I decided to make it a regular part of my grocery shopping list. However, it is not only important that you remain in control of what you eat, but to also be aware of any foods that could pose a problem for you in your weight loss effort. As I stated earlier, not everything that purports to be "low-carb" is necessarily good for you. Read the labels and decide for yourself what you can live with and still lose weight.

There are a few noted exceptions that can make your task of becoming carb-conscious a little bit easier. The products that have the Atkins-approved symbol on them (look for the big red "A") are usually the best ones for people watching their carbohydrate intake because they do not have any "hidden" sugars or unnecessary carbs in them. Many of these products are made by companies that got the Atkins seal of approval placed on them. The following are just a few of the low-carb food brands that I have used often during my weight loss and ones that I still use today:

Dreamfields Pasta - 5g net carbs per serving

Hood Carb Countdown Dairy Beverage - 2g net carbs for 8 oz glass

Atkins Multigrain Bread - 3g net carbs per slice

Carb Options Skippy Peanut Butter - 3g net carbs for 2 teaspoons

Atkins Breakfast and Meal Bars - 2-3g net carbs per bar

Z-Carb Chocolate Bars - 0g net carbs per bar

Russell Stover Low-Carb candies - 1-2g net carbs per package

Breyer's CarbSmart Ice Cream - 4 net carbs per serving

There are many other superb low-carb products available for you to choose from. These are some of the ones I used most often as I was losing weight on my low-carb program. Keep your eyes open for anything that may catch your attention that would be good for your low-carb lifestyle. The possibilities are endless.

I cannot overemphasize to you the fact that not everything claiming to be low-carb is actually low in carbohydrates. You can walk down just about any grocery aisle these days and see many products with words like "carb," "low-carb" or even "carb-free" in big, bold letters on them. While that will certainly catch your attention when you are trying to be carb-conscious, let that simply be your starting point to pick up the box and examine it for yourself to see if the carbohydrate content is low enough for you.

Speaking of the phrase "carb-free," let me dispel one of the myths about the low-carb way of eating. Low-carb does not mean "no carbs." Your body actually needs some carbohydrates to function. Yet most people simply eat many more carbohydrates than their body needs to function. All those extra carbs, mostly in the form of sugar, have contributed heavily to the obesity problem we have in the United States and around the world. That is why controlling your carb intake and becoming carb-conscious is the necessary foundation for beginning a low-carb lifestyle.

Being carb-conscious requires you to stay alert when you are food shopping so you can know for sure what you need to purchase while on a low-carb plan. This process has become so instinctive for me now that I don't even think about buying a food product without first looking at the nutritional label to see what the carbohydrate total is. Most people wouldn't buy something without knowing what the price of it is, right? Then why shouldn't the same strategy be used for the carbohydrate content of the foods you purchase. Otherwise, you are just asking for trouble as you attempt to do the low-carb lifestyle.

Don't worry if you accidentally get something that you later figure out that you shouldn't have. In addition to my incident with the hot dogs, I made a pretty big mistake when I first started on my low-carb lifestyle when I went to the corner convenience store to get a Diet Pepsi Vanilla on my way to church one day and inadvertently got the regular version instead. As soon as I took a big swig of it, I knew from the overwhelming sweetness in my mouth that I had gotten the wrong one. What did I do with the rest of it? Just like the hot dogs, I immediately threw it away because consuming that entire 20 oz. bottle would have blown my carb allowance for the entire week! I even counted that one swallow of sugar-filled Pepsi Vanilla in my carb journal as 12g carbs. I was so mad at myself for making such an avoidable mistake. But Pepsi didn't make it any easier on me by making the packaging of the diet and regular version of their soda look so similar. That's why you have to look carefully at everything you buy.

Speaking of a carb journal, this is an excellent way to keep track of how many carbohydrates you put into your body each day. Keep this journal handy with you at all times so you can register the amount of carbs, water and exercise you do on a daily basis.

For example:

CARBS
3+4+5+2+1=15

WATER
IIII (1.5 liter bottles)

EXERCISE
25 min on treadmill at 3.0 mph

This simple act of writing down every carb you consume allows you to visually see your progress and prevents you from going overboard on the amount of carbs you are allowed each day. I found this carb journal to be especially helpful as I began the process of becoming carb-conscious.

Once I had lost most of my weight, I was able to stop keeping a carb journal because it had become a permanent habit for me. Now I know exactly how many carbs I have eaten in a day without having to write it down. This dramatic transformation into carb-consciousness can and will take place the longer you stay on your low-carb lifestyle, which should be forever (as you will see in Chapter 10). Pretty soon, you will be well on your way to having your own low-carb weight loss success story to tell!

KEY POINTS TO REMEMBER FROM CHAPTER 1

- Stick with the Induction phase for the first two weeks

- Learn to count net carbs when shopping

- Continually educate yourself further about low-carb

- Choose only the low-carb foods you want to eat

- Stop dieting and start livin' la vida low-carb

- Feast on the buffet of food options awaiting you on low-carb

- Don't worry about fat or calories and focus on the net carbs

- Make sure you stay in ketosis by checking yourself often

- Read food labels carefully to insure what you buy is low-carb

- Keep a carb journal to help you become carb-conscious

Chapter 2
Water You Gonna Drink?

Don't scrunch up your nose like that at me because you know what you are about to read in this chapter is something you really need to hear. If you really want to possess an incredibly effective weight loss aid that will help you improve your overall health more than you can even imagine as you are livin' la vida low-carb, then you need to immediately start drinking a lot more water than you are right now.

EEEEEEEEEK!!!!

I know, I know, I can hear you now.

"Ugh!!! Water?! Are you kidding me? There's no way I could drink that stuff every single day in large quantities! After all, I get plenty of water intake from other drinks, so why do I have to drink plain old water? It's so gross! What's the big deal about water anyway?"

Breathe in ... breathe out ... breathe in ... breathe out ... Feel better now?

If any of those statements describe your opinion about water, then you are not alone. Actually, that little rant pretty much summed up my sentiment about water before I actually learned more about how that clear substance could help me reach my weight loss and overall health goals. If you want to quickly move forward into a new dimension of vastly improved health and accelerated weight loss, then you will not want to miss the message I have for you in this chapter.

You are probably thinking to yourself, "Why is water so important?" I'm glad you asked that question. Let's explore the answer fully over the next few pages.

We all know from high school chemistry class that water is two parts hydrogen, one part oxygen and comprises over half of your body and three-fourths of your muscles. Most people already know that your body simply cannot survive longer than just a few days without water or you will dehydrate and die. In case you've missed it, adequate daily water intake is incredibly important to maintaining optimum health by enabling your body to function as God intended.

However, when you are livin' la vida low-carb, it is that much more critical that you stay well-hydrated for a myriad of reasons that I will detail in this chapter. But first I have a challenge for you that will push you in a way that you have probably never been pushed before. Beginning right now even as you are reading this book, you need to start drinking water like your life depended on it. Ironically, for some of you it very well may. So start drinking up to your health!

Aw, man!

Once again I can hear you grumbling! Your first reaction to my challenge is probably along the lines of "yuck, water is so gross ... I don't see how you can expect me to drink that much water." My only response to you if this is how you feel is to reassure you that you will survive (I promise!), but you must do this if you want to lose that stubborn weight you've not been able to get rid of for years. There will be no ifs, ands or buts about it! Just do it and you will thank me later.

I don't care how you decide to do it, but you need to find a way to drink water that makes it more tolerable for you. Whether it is filtered, flavored or bottled, you need to start drinking more water. There are no excuses good enough to rationalize your way out of this one. If you need to add a lemon or a lime slice to your water so the taste will improve, then do it. There are also a plethora of flavored waters available on store shelves today, too. However, be careful to stay away from the ones that contain sugar and extra carbs, though. The last thing you need to add to your water intake is unnecessary carbs! That would be livin' la vida cuckoo!

If you live in an area of the country where the tap water tastes disgusting, then get a Brita filter or buy your favorite bottled water brand and drink as many as you can each and every day. Drink water with your meals and with snacks and you'll find that you will go through them very quickly. This may be a difficult transition for some people who are not used to drinking water, but it can and must be done.

Do you remember in the Introduction when I told you I used to drink about 200 ounces of soda daily before starting my low-carb lifestyle? Honestly, I'm surprised my body didn't go into some kind of sugar overload at some point or even develop diabetes because of it. Yet thank the good Lord nothing serious ever happened to my health and I was able to radically change my drinking habits before it was too late. I found that water quickly satisfied my thirst and filled that void that I used to attempt to satisfy with soda. As a result, my body has been the ultimate benefactor of that decision through unbelievable weight loss and improved health.

I consider myself fortunate because I have never had a problem with being thirsty. I have always been able to drink a lot of liquids. In fact, my wife has been worried about me becoming a diabetic since a strong thirst is one indicator of having that condition. But by the grace of God I have never been diagnosed with diabetes.

But I have to laugh when my wife and I go out to a restaurant to eat because I always seem to have a difficult time getting the server to keep my drink glass full while I am there. I always warn them ahead of time that I'm a "heavy drinker" with a grin, but they quickly discover that I mean that literally. After the server refills my glass for the third time during the first ten minutes of my visit, I think she finally realizes she needs to keep an eye on my glass. In fact, some restaurants we visit often bring me two or three glasses to drink right away knowing I will go through them very quickly. My reputation for drinking a lot precedes me.

Before I started on my low-carb lifestyle, the primary problem I encountered trying to deal with my high thirst level was what I was drinking to quench that thirst. Unfortunately, for most of us, we choose to drink anything and everything but plain water. For me it was sugar-laced sodas. For others, it could be coffee, tea or alcoholic beverages. Unfortunately, these can and will cause problems which I will explain in this chapter.

If we know it is good for us, then why don't we drink more water than we do? It's not like clean drinking water is in scarce supply. It is everywhere around us, in fountains, faucets and even in bottles. Over the next few pages, I will attempt to provide you with several reasons why drinking water is absolutely necessary and hopefully give you a sense of urgency about wanting to drink more of it right away as you are beginning your low-carb lifestyle.

Drinking water may be hard for you at first, but it will become easier and easier the more you do it. If you have never been on a regular water drinking plan before, then be prepared for a new experience unlike anything you have ever done before. But take it from someone who has been through it, you will soon have a desire to drink more water and even have a smile on your face about it! No kidding! More importantly, beginning a regular water schedule will help you kick your low-carb lifestyle into high gear and the benefits are plentiful. Also be sure to start keeping track of your daily water intake by adding it to the carb journal I talked about at the end of Chapter 1.

My friends and co-workers affectionately call me "Waterboy" like the Adam Sandler movie character a few years ago. My favorite line from the comedy flick is when the Sandler character exclaims after drinking some extra-purified water, "That's some high-quality H2O."

Every time people see me I'm carrying around a big bottle of water. I wear that "Waterboy" label proudly because I know I am healthier because of it. I like carrying around those gigantic 1 1/2 liter bottles and refilling them when they get empty because they are a powerful visual reminder that I need to drink a lot of water. Let me tell you, I can put away some water! But it wasn't always that easy for me.

When I first started on my low-carb program, I had to force myself to drink about 4-6 of these 1 1/2 liter bottles each and every day. When I say forced, I mean I held my nose and literally shoved those bottles into my mouth kickin' and screamin' all the way. Needless to say, it was extremely difficult getting used to the taste and interesting side effects of drinking that much water in a day. But it quickly became as routine for me as eating low-carb foods did. In fact, now I don't even think about guzzling down a few 1 1/2 liter bottles of water every single day because it's a good habit that I have developed and keeps me healthy.

Water is such an essential component to a healthy body because it helps carry the nutrients, oxygen and waste products to their appropriate place. Additionally, it cools the body which is especially important when you are packing on a few extra pounds. I know this because I was once there.

If you are severely obese or overweight, then you are probably a hot-natured person. I know I was extremely hot all the time when

I was 410 pounds and I would sweat profusely. My wife never had to ask me if she could turn down the air-conditioner at home. If she was starting to get hot, then I had already been sweltering for quite some time! It was miserable for both of us because she would always be too cold while I would simultaneously be too hot.

There would even be days when I would come home from work and my shirt would be literally soaking wet because my underarms would sweat so much. What a disgusting sight that was! Also, my hands would stay so clammy all the time because of the perspiration that developed from being so hot. I was afraid to shake anyone's hand because I didn't want them to deal with touching my nasty sweaty palms. I constantly drank soda to try to cool my body down, but obviously that was not the answer.

Amazingly, after starting a water drinking program to complement my low-carb lifestyle, I noticed I would not get as hot as I used to and my underarms and hands stopped getting sweaty. As the weight began to lose, my body temperature came way down as well causing my hands and feet to become as cold as ice. I freak people out all the time when they feel how cold my hands are, especially in the morning when I drink the most water. Now the tables have now turned with my wife and me. She's the one who stays hot and I'm the one who is always cold. Go figure!

When I say you need to drink more water, I am of course referring to plain water. The water you get from other sources in beverages like tea, coffee, soda and even food is important, but you should not count them towards your daily water intake because they only provide a nominal amount of water. You really need to drink plain water to help your body run more efficiently.

Did you know you are less likely to have kidney stones and certain types of cancer if you drink a lot of water? The healing effects that come from the oxygen in water help protect your body from these and other harmful ailments. It is such a shame that so many diseases could be easily prevented if we would just drink more water. Why is it that we choose not to drink more water when we know is good for us to drink? This must be one of life's many mysteries.

For the person livin' la vida low-carb, there are several weight loss benefits associated with getting an ample amount of water in your body. It can act as an appetite suppressant and it can help flush the body of excess fat. Those are good things, don't you think? Conversely, an inadequate amount of water intake will actually cause fat deposits in your body to dramatically increase. Yikes! If you needed just one good reason to drink more water, then there it is!

Furthermore, your kidneys need enough water to properly flush out all the impurities and toxins in your body. If water is scarce in the body, then the liver has to perform some of the work of the kidneys. When this happens, the liver is prevented from doing its primary function of transforming stored fat into energy. If less stored fat is metabolized because the liver is busy helping the kidneys, then weight loss can and will come to an immediate halt. That's not a good thing when you are trying to lose weight!

Interestingly, the body can become extraordinarily stubborn when it doesn't get enough water. If it receives less water than it needs, then it will go into survival mode and hold on to every single drop of water it has. The body will store this water in the feet, legs and hands because it is attempting to preserve itself from becoming completely dehydrated. This water weight will rapidly build up in your system and, thus, greatly hinder your weight loss. Once again, this is not good.

But the solution to this problem is so incredibly simple. Drink more water!!! There is no magic pill or secret ingredient. Just drink more water. When you do, the stored water in your body will immediately be released and the regular bodily functions will return to normal, which is healthy for the body. Like the radiator in your car, if you keep it filled with water and antifreeze so that it never gets low, then your car will run like it is supposed to and not get overheated or worse. In the same way your body is able to perform at maximum capacity when you stay well-hydrated.

When you carry around excessive weight like I did, drinking more water becomes that much more important. A larger person generally has a lot slower metabolism as well as loads of stored fat to get rid of. Weighing in at 410 pounds when I started the low-carb lifestyle, I knew I needed to drink a lot more water than the average person did. So I started to chug-a-lug water like it was going out of style! Gulp, gulp, gulp, gulp.

Besides helping you with your weight loss, your muscles and skin will thank you for drinking more water, too. A healthy and clear complexion will result and your muscles will become toned. Your blood circulation will improve as well. My co-worker Mary is always complimenting me on how healthy my fingernails look because she can see how pink they are from the proper blood flow in my body. The high amount of water that I drink causes this to happen.

For the person trying to lose weight, the absolute best benefit that water provides is the way it naturally rids the body of excess waste and stored fat. I know just talking about this sounds gross already, but look at it as a positive sign of success when you are on a low-carb plan. That stored fat has to be flushed out of the body somehow and water will certainly do the trick. You will notice a huge difference in what comes out of your body in the form of waste as the body goes into this process generated by a high water consumption.

I'm not going to lie to you, some of your first few trips to the bathroom will be very difficult in the beginning days and weeks of your increased water intake. The bigger you are, the more your body will want and need to get rid of a lot of waste. It'll be an excruciating experience in the short term, but your body will be glad to be rid of these toxins that have threatened to ruin your health for so many years. I encourage you to get excited when this happens because you will literally be able to see you body purging itself of the stored fat that has haunted you over your entire life.

One of the problems people can experience on a low-carb lifestyle that is easily remedied by consuming more water is constipation. If you drink the amount of water I have suggested in this chapter, then you will not be constipated. Trust me on this. It would be virtually impossible for you to be constipated if you are drinking as much water as you should. I will talk about the importance of adding more fiber to your body in Chapter 4 when I discuss important supplements that can also assist you with constipation. But you will notice your bowel functioning at its optimum level when you start drinking plenty of water.

Exercise and warmer weather affect the amount of water you need to drink, too. In the summer and during moderate to heavy exercise, drink at least 1-2 more bottles of water to replenish the loss of fluids that naturally happens during these times. By the way, don't think you're gonna get out of exercising while you are on the low-carb lifestyle. We'll tackle that subject in the next chapter. Happy thoughts, happy thoughts.

A key point to remember regarding water is to simply make sure you are always drinking enough of it so you are never thirsty. If you ever feel even the least bit thirsty, then you are probably already dehydrated. Keep sipping away at your water all day so this never happens. Again, it may be hard for you at first, but it most certainly gets a lot easier and more routine in no time.

Okay, so perhaps I have convinced you to start drinking more water. You might be wondering, "Now what's going to happen?" Once you get into a regular daily water drinking schedule, you will notice an immediate reaction. You will quickly realize you need to go to the bathroom a lot more frequently than you are probably used to. Let me tell you now that this is completely normal and your water drinking plan should not be abandoned because of it. In fact, it's a good sign that you are finally getting enough water for your body to function correctly.

During these crucial early days of drinking more water, your body will almost immediately react by releasing all that water it has been storing up in your body during survival mode because it will sense a return to normalcy and balance. If you haven't been drinking an adequate amount of water for a long time, then it may take a while for your body to completely flush out all of this water build-up. Again, this is normal and you should not be alarmed. This intensive process of cleansing the body of stored water will prepare you for even greater weight loss as you start livin' la vida low-carb.

In fact, you may even notice some parts of your body that have become swollen from the stored water return to their normal size after you start drinking more water. This is a positive sign of your body relinquishing the water it was storing in body parts such as your ankles, hips and thighs because it will sense a return to normal water intake. Survival mode will cease and your body will get back to the way it was intended to function.

But there is a nemesis that is counterproductive to drinking more water. That evil opponent is caffeine. Consuming large amounts of caffeine not only dehydrates you, but also increases your heart rate, makes you crave sweets because it causes your blood sugar to drop, and dramatically slows the metabolic rate. All of these things are counterproductive to weight loss.

That is why I recommend that you stay away from drinking coffee, tea and diet sodas that have caffeine in them. It is just not worth the struggle to consume something that will slow the progress of your weight loss. It would be like running a marathon with 20-pound ankle weights on each leg. You could still do it, but it takes a little longer and a lot more effort to reach the finish line. Of course, that's assuming you don't get discouraged and quit first.

I highly recommend that you get a caffeine-free, Splenda-flavored diet soda if you absolutely need to have a carbonated beverage to drink. My favorite brands are Diet Rite and Diet Cheerwine and both are readily available at most grocery stores. In fact, they are probably the best known brands that have Splenda and are caffeine-free. The Diet Rite brand comes in the original Cola, Tangerine, Red Raspberry, Kiwi- Strawberry, Black Cherry and White Grape flavors. There is also a superb selection of flavors in a line of diet sodas called Waist Watcher (www.waist-watcher.com). However, the distribution of this particular brand is not as widespread as Diet Rite and Cheerwine.

The reason these diet sodas are better for you is because they are sweetened with Splenda, the preferred sugar-substitute when you are livin' la vida low-carb. I'll explain in a later chapter why Splenda is better than other artificial sweeteners such as Equal and Sweet & Low and is obviously a lot better for you to consume than sugar.

But up until early 2005, the major soda companies had long failed to realize how important Splenda is to those of us on a low-carb lifestyle. Finally, though, after a lot of proverbial arm-twisting and pleas from people doing a low-carb lifestyle, both Coke and Pepsi came out with Splenda-flavored options for their customers. Pepsi One with Splenda was released in March and Diet Coke with Splenda hit the market in May. While these companies are finally beginning to show an interest in satisfying the needs of people who are livin' la vida low-carb, they are still moving at a lot slower speed in developing the flavors we want with the ingredients we need and don't need.

Of course, both Pepsi and Coke still sell their original diet soda versions made with aspartame, aka the brand name Nutrasweet. I have found that consuming a lot of aspartame can cause me to have massive headaches and I personally believe it tastes much worse than Splenda-flavored diet soft drinks do. Furthermore, most of the diet sodas on the market, including the new Diet Coke with Splenda and Coke Zero (made with aspartame too, by the way!), still have caffeine in them (as of the writing of this book, a caffeine-free version of Diet Coke with Splenda had not been introduced). It's yet another sign that the major food and beverage companies still don't get it. But they are trying, I guess.

Another detrimental drink standing in the way of your getting enough water intake is alcoholic beverages. These are not only bad for your health for a myriad of reasons besides causing dehydration, but they also stall your weight loss because they literally suck the water out of your body and cause internal problems that you don't want to experience. To borrow a phrase from a famous public service announcement, friends don't let friends drink and diet!

Hopefully you have learned in this chapter that water should be your first priority when it comes to drinking. It should be consumed throughout the day by constantly having it on hand to drink at all times. That may sound like a big chore, but it will do your body a lot of good.

There is also an excellent selection of low-carb milk and juices to choose from when you need a break from drinking water. Use these sparingly and be careful about consuming too many carbs in your low-carb beverage choices. If you drink a big bottle of water for every glass of a low-carb beverage, then you should be fine.

It goes without saying, but whatever you do, stop drinking water at least three hours before you go to bed. There's nothing more uncomfortable than "gotta go, gotta go, gotta go right now," throughout the night. You may experience the urge to get up during the night often when you first start your water drinking schedule because of the stored water releasing, but it will subside once this water is flushed through your system.

By the way, keep an eye on the color of your urine. The only time it should ever be yellow is when you first get up in the morning or after taking your vitamins. Otherwise, it should be relatively clear. Use the urine test often to determine if you are getting enough water.

Let me reiterate the importance of water when you are livin' la vida low-carb. If you do not get enough water, your weight loss will slow down or stop completely, you will not be able to digest the foods you are eating, you will feel like you are very hungry when in fact your body will be very thirsty, and you will hinder the benefits that exercise gives your body. Why wouldn't you drink as much water as you can to prevent these things from happening?

Here are a few final tips for getting enough water in your body each and every day while doing a low-carb lifestyle:

- Keep plenty of water on hand at all times and sip on it often

- Carry at least one water bottle with you at all times

- Reward yourself after drinking water by having a caffeine-free diet soda

- Eat spicy or slightly-salted foods that will cause you to drink more water
- Drink a bottle of water on each of the commutes to and from work

Now that you are better educated about how important the wet stuff is for you, water you gonna drink? The answer should be obvious now.

KEY POINTS TO REMEMBER FROM CHAPTER 2:

- Start drinking water like you have never drunk it before
- Get your water filtered, flavored or bottled if the tap tastes terrible
- Drink 4-6 1 1/2 liter bottles of water daily
- Only count plain water in your daily water intake
- Let your liver metabolize stored fat by drinking more water
- Don't ever get thirsty by constantly sipping on water throughout the day
- Stick with the drinking plan evan as your body rids itself of excess waste
- Stay away from drinks with caffeine and alcohol in them
- Stop drinking water at least three hours before bedtime
- Check your urine often to see if you are getting enough water intake

Chapter 3
Exercise Is Not A Dirty Word

As much as you probably despised the subject matter of the previous chapter, I am almost sure this chapter on the subject of exercise isn't going to thrill you too much either. Nevertheless, I'm going to try to convince you that exercise is not a dirty word. I know you don't believe me now, but it's not. You'll see.

It wasn't that long ago that the subject of exercise was an entirely foreign concept to me. I had never purposefully engaged in any kind of a regular, daily exercise routine ever in my entire life before 2004. Never! I just didn't have the will nor the desire to invest even just a few minutes each day to move my body and make it sweat. Why should I bother because it hurts too much and it doesn't do any good anyway? At least that's what I thought before I started livin' la vida low-carb.

Am I ringing a familiar bell here? Is this possibly a description of how you may feel about exercise? Does it just seem like a one big chore and you don't think you have enough time and energy to devote to exercising every single day? Do you sincerely believe you'll never be fit enough to exercise as much as you should?

If you answered yes to any or all of those questions, then you definitely need to keep reading to learn how I transformed my body from the extremely sluggish, out-of-shape, lazy couch potato destined for a one-way ticket to the grave, into the lean, mean exercising machine, full of energy and lover of life that I am today!

What is so incredibly amazing about my radical mindset transformation regarding exercise is that I never would have thought the process of becoming a regular exerciser would be as easy as it was. Oh, don't get me wrong, it was a lot of hard work when I first began and it still pushes my body to this day. But if you told me before 2004 that I would be exercising every single day and actually wanting to do it because my body craved it, then I would have thought you were completely nuts! But exercise is as much a part of my life now as brushing my teeth (in case you were wondering, yes, I do that every day, too!).

I began my new exercise routine one month after I started my low-carb lifestyle in February 2004. I had just lost about 30 pounds on my new eating lifestyle and was confident my eating habits were on the right track for considerable weight loss. But I knew I needed to do more than simply change the way I ate to get my body into the tip-top shape it needed to be in. That's when I turned to what I thought was the dirtiest word in the English language -- exercise!

Instinctively, I started incorporating exercise into my weight loss plan because I knew it was going to be a necessary ingredient to my success. Isn't it funny how we know in our heads how much we need to exercise, but somehow we rationalize away why we can't do it? I guess we can chalk this one up as another one of life's little mysteries!

Since I get a free membership to the YMCA as a part of my benefits package at work, I decided to take full advantage of this company benefit by dedicating myself to daily cardiovascular training. Yes, I said daily, as in every day of the week. That means Saturdays and Sundays, too. I vowed that I needed to do this every single day of every week as an immediate goal when I started my new exercise routine. Was I crazy? Probably a little, but I was determined to do this no matter how much it hurt me physically or mentally.

About a year later, after I had lost the majority of my weight, I decided to add weight lifting exercises to my workout schedule because I knew building muscle would help my body burn more fat and help tone areas that needed firming up. Once again, I knew this was something I needed to do as I was losing weight, but I just didn't do it.

Now that I look back on my weight loss experience in hindsight, I wish I had also started my strength-building exercises at the same time I started my cardiovascular exercises. I will explain later in this chapter why my decision against starting my weight lifting program was probably not the best idea for me and why it is important for you to combine your cardio workouts with strength training.

Now we interrupt this chapter for an important message from the author:

Let me take just a brief moment to comment on the YMCA. This place is a real godsend for people wanting to improve their health and fitness. Located in virtually every community across the United States, the local YMCA gives people an excellent environment to workout and engage their body in healthy exercise activities without the embarrassment associated with what I like to refer to as "boutique" gyms. I think you know the ones I'm describing! The people I have encountered at several YMCA facilities across the country have been nothing but top-notch professionals who care deeply about their members' physical and spiritual health needs and are dedicated to helping those of us seeking to improve our overall health. To find the YMCA nearest to you, please visit them on the Internet at www.ymca.net.

Now we join your regularly scheduled chapter already in progress...

If you are not currently doing any exercise at all, then you need to get on an exercise routine as soon as possible. The benefits to your overall health cannot be overstated. Additionally, since you are primarily trying to lose weight at this point, you will quickly see tremendous results by committing yourself to a regular time of daily exercise.

There are a couple of common misconceptions floating around out there by so-called health experts and diet gurus that state, "You don't have to exercise if you are on a low-carb program" or even more ridiculous notion such as "you shouldn't exercise while on a low-carb eating plan." These ill-advised statements are utterly ridiculous and dangerously wrong! If you are doing any kind of effective weight loss program, then exercise should always be an automatic prerequisite. But not everyone has always thought this way, myself included.

When I lost 170 pounds on a low-fat diet in 1999, do you realize not once did I ever do any kind of exercise during that weight loss? Absolutely zero, zilch, zippo. It didn't even cross my mind the entire time I was losing weight. In fact, I remember how much I used to brag about how I did not do one single exercise to complement my low-fat diet. I even gloated about it as if I had achieved something great by not exercising! Man, I look back on that now and think, "How could I have been so stupid!" After I gained back all that weight I had lost and then some, I learned an incredibly valuable lesson that finally took hold when I started livin' la vida low-carb in 2004. Exercise is a must when it comes to losing and maintaining your weight as well as improving your overall health.

Now I proudly admit to anyone and everyone who will listen to me that exercise has played a key role in my low-carb weight loss success story. There is no way I would have been nearly as successful as I was without the benefits I receive from daily exercise. I absolutely love walking the treadmill, doing the elliptical machine, working up a sweat on the Stairmaster, shooting basketball, playing volleyball and just about any other fun activity that will increase my heart rate and make me sweat. I've committed myself 100% to exercising every single day for the rest of my life so I can keep my body as healthy as it can be as I'm livin' la vida low-carb!

But how much exercise is enough when you are just starting out and barely have the energy to do even one sit-up a day? There's a famous Christian comedian named Mark Lowry who said a few years ago in a comedy skit that he does one sit-up a day -- when he gets up in the morning, that's half; and when he lies down at night, that's the other half! Whatever you decide to do, though, don't expect the government to provide you with an encouraging answer to the question about how much exercise is enough.

In response to the growing obesity problem in America, the Department of Health and Human Services released their new "Dietary Guidelines for Americans" in early 2005 which recommended Americans need to be getting a minimum of 30 minutes of exercise per day to be in good health. As someone who was once new to exercise, I don't believe it's unreasonable for people to start at that level so they can get into the habit of exercising to improve their health. Unfortunately, though, that recommendation was only intended for people who are considered slim and in generally good health.

If you are overweight, obese or experience any detrimental health problems associated with too much weight, the American government recommends that you get 60-90 minutes of exercise per day to lose and maintain your weight loss. I can hear you screaming again. You're thinking, "Say what? There is no way in the world I'll be able to do that much exercise. That's just asking too much." Now hang on for a second and let me explain my thoughts about this. Before you throw this book down in absolute disgust thinking there's no way you'll ever be able to do that much exercise in just one day, much less every single day, keep reading. It's going to get better, I promise.

Your first reaction to this "recommendation" by the government regarding exercise is probably something along the lines of "That's completely absurd! What normal person exercises that much in a day? How can I do that much exercise with all this weight I have on my body?" Looking at your situation in light of your current weight and probable sedentary lifestyle at face value, I would completely agree with you.

But (you knew there had to be a "but," didn't you?)...

Since I began an exercise program in early 2004, I have seen firsthand the benefits of getting a minimum of 45-60 minutes per day of a good cardiovascular workout and eventually adding another 30-45 minutes per day of a strength building workout as part of my successful weight loss and weight maintenance plan. While that may seem like a long time to people who are not used to exercising, it really does not take very long before your body will actually want and need the 60-90 minutes per day as a minimum.

There are some days I can get up to 120-180 minutes of workout time when I make the time to fit it into my schedule and feel the need to extend my routine when I'm feeling especially good. You will find that your body will begin to crave exercise more and more just like it used to crave hot fudge cake before you started livin' la vida low-carb! I'm serious!

One excuse I often hear people give me about not exercising enough is that their schedule is so full that they don't have time to fit it in. You know what, if you are that busy, then you need to cut out some activities in your life to make the time for exercise. Your life literally depends upon your making the right choices right now in order to get you body into shape for the sake of your health and future.

Whether it is before work, during lunch or after work, you must make the time to exercise. Isn't it amazing how we can schedule just about everything else in the world into our lives, but we can't seem to find the time for even a few minutes of exercise? There are no excuses allowed -- you just need to do it! This is not negotiable if you want to succeed at losing weight.

Don't let that government standard of 60-90 minutes per day scare you away from doing any exercise at all. I am concerned that this recommendation by the government will only lead to frustration for people who are battling weight problems and will likely cause more people to give up altogether on doing any kind of exercise program. I am afraid this will only lead people who are overweight and obese to continue packing on even more pounds in the coming years.

I know the government had good intentions with its recommended health standards, but I contend they have no business getting involved in this issue because it is a personal problem that must be confronted by individuals. Common sense tells you that you need to start an exercise routine at your own pace and eventually work your way up to a level you are comfortable with. We do not need the government telling us what kind and how much exercise we need. That decision should be ours alone.

Even if you just start off doing 30 minutes of walking on the treadmill at a reasonable pace, then do it every day and make it a regular part of your life. This lifestyle change will give you nearly instantaneous results as you begin to feel better physically with your newly invigorated and energized body. Your body will gradually transform itself into the athlete you never knew existed underneath all that skin of yours!

I started exercising every single day as part of my low-carb lifestyle and I consider it an integral part of my weight loss and weight maintenance success. You are simply depriving your body of so many health benefits if you do not incorporate regular exercise into your weight loss efforts. Pretty soon you will find that 30 minutes per day is not nearly enough.

From day one of my new workout schedule, I committed myself to exercise every day of the week at the gym during my lunch break (which was good because it took my mind off of food!). If you decide against joining a gym or using exercise equipment, then find a walking path or track in your area where you can do a structured cardio workout. Make sure you get into a regular routine so you will not stray from the plan. This is extremely important to ensure you will successfully meet you fitness goals.

It was a daunting task for my severely overweight body and, honestly, it will not be easy for you either. But nothing worth achieving ever happens without a lot of hard work. Always remember in the back of your mind while you are exercising that this is something you need to do if you are going to be serious about your weight loss. It is just as important as watching your carb intake. Livin' la vida low-carb isn't easy at first, but the proven results make it all worth it in the end.

I remember the first day I stepped on the treadmill downstairs at the downtown Spartanburg, South Carolina YMCA in this little room full of cardio exercise equipment with about ten television sets. I affectionately called this place "The Dungeon" because it was downstairs away from civilization. But I would grow to love "The Dungeon" because it was the birthing place of my new and improved body.

My body composition compared with the other people in "The Dungeon" when I first started going was much more flabby and a lot less able to move than theirs was. But, deep down inside of me I had the grit and sheer determination to not remain where I was physically. I was destined to change my life forever and it all started with that first step on the treadmill.

I can vividly remember when I began the very first workout of my entire life that I was on the treadmill at 3.0 miles per hour for 20 minutes. I was literally drenched in sweat and felt completely worn out when I was finished walking that day. But it was great knowing this was such a breakthrough moment in my life. Never again would I be that sluggish, fat guy who struggled to walk just one flight of stairs without gasping for air. I was well on my way to becoming as fit as an athlete! Me, an athlete? It eventually happened for me and it can happen for you, too!

Over those first few weeks and months, I slowly increased my speed on the treadmill from 3.0 up to 3.5 and even pushed it to 4.0 to see how long I could sustain my walking at that speed. The total amount of time I stayed on the treadmill also increased to 30-45 minutes and eventually would last as long as an hour. As your body becomes more conditioned to working out, you are able to go faster and faster for longer periods of time. You know your body best and can adjust the speed and length of time you exercise according to how much you can handle.

Just as you did with your carb and water intake, make sure you journal the kind and amount of exercise you do each day in your journal. This was probably what helped me more than anything else to remain encouraged as I noticed my speed and length of time doing cardio get faster and longer as the weeks and months progressed. You need that visual reminder that you are doing well to stay motivated to get into shape.

But there was a moment when I almost quit exercising for good because the pain was beginning to be too much for me to bear. What pain, you ask? Well, for me, it was blisters, and not just little ones either. These were the biggest blisters I have ever seen in my entire life lined all along the bottom of my feet. On my heels, on my toes and on the balls of my feet, these painful reminders that I had chosen to exercise would probably have caused most people to stop. I will admit that I was tempted to stop on several occasions.

As I look back on my experience with the blisters now, I realize I probably could have avoided all that pain if I had been wearing shoes that comfortably fit my feet. I had no idea that part of my weight loss was in my feet and my shoe size had literally changed in just a few short months! Because my shoes had become loose, the constant slipping of my foot inside my shoe caused the blisters to form.

What kept me going when my body wanted to give up?

In a word -- motivation. I don't just give up on something that easily without a fight. I will discuss in greater detail about my personal motivation during this weight loss experience in Chapter 5, but I want to share with you a quick story that illustrates just how motivated I had become when it came to exercising.

I can remember my blisters hurting so bad one day several months after I started my new exercise routine at the gym that I could barely walk. It literally felt like I was walking on sharp pieces of glass as the pain shot through my entire body with each new step. But I reasoned in my mind that I had come too far to give up now and I wasn't about to abandon my desire to get healthy. Call it what you want, but I prayed that God would strengthen me during this difficult and pivotal moment in my weight loss endeavor. To the glory of the Lord, He did just that in the most remarkable way.

Thinking back on this experience now, I can laugh about the many strange looks I received on that day that I wanted to give up. You see, when I stepped up on the treadmill, I began walking in the most peculiar manner that I could have ever come up with. There I was with the bottom soles of my shoes literally pointing inward towards each other as I limped my way for 30 minutes on that piece of exercise equipment -- walking on the sides of my shoes! I did not care how silly it looked to anyone because my feet were hurting and nothing was going to stop me from reaching my weight loss goals.

I have to chuckle now when I think about that day I walked on the sides of my feet because I can only imagine how stupid it made me look at the time. But I also feel a sense of pride that God gave me the strength and desire to do that and not abandon my ultimate goal of losing weight and getting healthy. This was another turning point in my weight loss story because it showed me that I was willing to deal with a little temporary pain now to reach my goals.

The only other pain I experienced while exercising, other than occasional muscle soreness, was an annoying rash that developed on both of my inner thighs. When I was larger than I am now, my thighs got to know each other very well by being in such close proximity. In fact, I would sometimes hear them talking to each other as I walked. "Excuse me, pardon me, excuse me, pardon me..."

All joking aside, with my thighs rubbing up against each other, it was inevitable that a rash would develop and try to slow me down. Some days I would have to walk like a cowboy who had just ridden a horse for twelve hours straight. But just like the blisters, I kept on walking through the pain knowing my thighs will eventually stop touching and rubbing each other raw. They did, but once again the pain from the rash could have stopped me from continuing on!

Eventually the rash went away and those blisters began to heal and harden up. In no time, I was able to boost my treadmill speed to 4.5 miles per hour for an average of 60-90 minutes a day. But after walking on the treadmill for 7 months, I knew it was time to graduate to the next level of equipment -- the elliptical machine.

I tried the elliptical machine once early on in my weight loss, but I couldn't do it at any speed for more than 5 minutes without absolutely collapsing from exhaustion. It is quite a workout. But now the elliptical machine, as well as the Stairmaster on occasion, have become my preferred methods of cardio exercise. It's not unusual for me to do a 60 minute cardiovascular workout at 8.0-9.0 miles per hour on the elliptical machine. Who would have ever thought that I would come this far when I first started out at 3.0 miles per hour for 20 minutes on the treadmill and gasping for air? Now I barely break a sweat in the first 20 minutes on the elliptical.

Despite the minor bump in the road I experienced with the blisters and rash, it wasn't that hard to get to the next level of fitness once I started doing a regular exercise routine. The most important part was getting into the habit of doing it and sticking with it.

What about you? Are you frightened at the prospect of starting an exercise plan? Is exercise really a dirty word for you? Let me provide you with a little more information that may help make your decision a little easier about whether or not you should start exercising.

A moderate cardiovascular workout combined with a low-carb lifestyle is a powerful combination to get your body into optimal condition. You bring more oxygen to your blood and you burn a lot of fat when you exercise. When you are livin' la vida low-carb, stored fat is transformed into the energy that you need to make it through your workout! Despite what you may hear from people attempting to discourage you from starting an exercise routine in combination with your low-carb plan, your body will feel more energized and alive from daily moderate exercise than it ever has before. I didn't think it was possible to enjoy exercise, but I am living proof that it can and will happen if you give it a chance to work!

In fact, a University of Illinois study published in the August 2005 issue of the Journal of Nutrition found that exercise is much more effective and helps to lower triglyceride levels when it's coupled with a protein-rich diet while a higher-carbohydrate, lower-protein diet based on the USDA food guide pyramid actually reduced the benefits of exercise. That's great news for people who are livin' la vida low-carb!

Another benefit that comes from exercising, besides more energy and endurance, is it will keep you going even when your weight loss hits a wall. Say what?! What wall?! We'll talk about perseverance during these challenging times when weight loss stops in a Chapter 9, but all you need to know is that exercise plays a key role in getting you through those times when you struggle.

I've got a great secret to share with you about the difference between people who are on a low-carb program and exercise vs. those who do a low-fat diet and exercise. Low-fat supporters don't want you to know this, but did you know it takes 20 minutes of continuous cardiovascular exercise to start burning stored fat if you are on a low-fat diet because you body first has to burn the sugar and other carbohydrates in your body before it can burn the stored fat? But when you exercise while following a low-carb lifestyle, your body immediately begins to burn stored fat during those first 20 minutes and beyond because you don't have the extra sugar or carbohydrates in your body to burn. Did you get that?! You burn stored fat as soon as you start exercising when you mix low-carb with your cardio workout! Woo hoo! What this means is your 20-minute workout is just as effective as the 40-minute workout that a low-fat dieter does! Suckers!

Whatever you do, though, make sure you eat something before you workout. Don't go pigging out within an hour of going to exercise, but make sure you aren't ravenously hungry when you go or you won't make it through your routine without physically collapsing. Eat a light low-carb snack and then go to the gym energized and ready to lose that stored fat!

Remember when I noted earlier that I wish I had added strength building exercises to my workout routine sooner? I had my reasons at the time for staying away from bodybuilding while trying to lose weight. But looking back on those excuses I made now, none of them were legitimate reasons to avoid weight training early on in my weight loss plan.

First, I thought it would be counterproductive to my weight loss. I had always heard that you gain more weight when you build muscle because it weighs more than fat does. Since my goal was to lose weight, I did not understand why I needed to do something that would cause me to gain weight. But the tradeoff for me would have been that my body would have burned even more fat and calories by speeding up my metabolism and it would have been better for me in the long run had I begun lifting weights.

Second, I didn't think I could endure both a cardio and weight lifting workout simultaneously. Again, this was a poor excuse for not building my strength as well. If only I had started lifting weights sooner, I would have been able to shape and tone parts of my body that now have a lot of excess skin on them. This problem may not have been as pronounced as it is now, especially in my abdomen and thighs, if I had begun muscle training at the same time I started my cardio workouts.

Third, I believed building muscle would make my body ache too much and discourage me from continuing with my exercise program. While my body certainly went through its fair share of soreness and pain during some of my cardiovascular workouts, adding strength training exercises would not have caused me to have that much more pain and it was just an excuse that I used to rationalize not doing it.

Let me tell you something, though. When I started lifting weights for the first time in my life beginning in March 2005 after losing 180 pounds, something remarkable began to happen. My energy level, which was already soaring from the weight loss, continued to skyrocket. I was able to sleep better without the tossing and turning that used to plague me when I was out of shape. The bonus for me was when my wife noticed all the muscles that started to pop out in my arms and legs that she never knew existed under all that fat! Now I'm her hunka hunka burning hubby, baby! Hoooooooo!

What's really amazing is how much progress can be made in just a short amount of time. If you devote just three to five days a week to strength building exercises while doing your daily cardio, the results will be unbelievable for you. People will take notice as your weight drops and your muscles begin to emerge. That healthy body you've always wanted is just screaming to come out!

I highly recommend you speak with a certified trainer and your physician before starting any kind of strength building or cardiovascular routine. There may be some limitations you need to be aware of due to the needs of your individual body. But most people are able to do at least a moderate workout on a regular basis to get their bodies into shape.

My trainer started me out working two parts of my body, three times a week. I would do my arms and chest on day one, skip a day, my shoulders and back on day two, skip a day, and my legs on day three. Additionally, I would work my abs and calves on each of the days I did strength training exercise.

After just six weeks I not only noticed a huge difference in my strength and began adding more weight to my workouts, but I also increased the frequency of my weight lifting. Be sure you don't work the same muscle group in consecutive days, though, because you could cause injury to your body. Again, let a personal trainer monitor your progress to help you determine when it is time to graduate to the next level. Weight lifting has improved my health that much more and I don't know what I would do without it now.

Once you start working out on a regular basis, you will always want to be at the gym doing more and more to get your body into the best shape it can be. My only word of caution for you is to listen to your body and stop if you feel extreme pain or dizziness. Otherwise, as Hanz and Franz used to say on Saturday Night Live, "It's time to pump you up!"

See, I told you exercise wasn't a dirty word after all!

KEY POINTS TO REMEMBER FROM CHAPTER 3:

- Join a gym or find a regular walking trail you can use
- Start your cardio workout slowly and gradually increase the speed
- Don't listen to people who tell you not to exercise and eat low-carb
- Find exercise activities you enjoy, such as basketball or volleyball
- Work your way up to 60-90 minutes per day of exercise

- Stay committed to the workout even when it hurts
- Start burning stored fat immediately when you exercise on low-carb
- Begin strength training exercises for muscle tone
- Watch your energy soar and burn more fat when you exercise
- Consult a certified trainer and your physician before starting your exercise routine

Chapter 4
Vitamins Vital For Vitality

When you talk about vitamins, some people immediately cringe when they hear that word because of all the negative connotations it may conjure up in their minds. That Christian comedian I told you about earlier named Mark Lowry put it best in a comedy sketch when he said, "Have you ever bitten into a vitamin? It tastes awful because it's got vitamins in it!"

We can all remember when we were forced by our parents to choke down foods that were supposedly good for us when we were children because of their alleged vitamin content. Unfortunately, though, over time the vitamin content in foods has changed dramatically from what it used to be. Did you know the amount of vitamins and minerals found in foods nowadays is virtually nonexistent?

Even in so-called healthy foods like fruits and vegetables, the lack of adequate nutritional content is simply astounding. Nutritionists say even if you ate raw fruits and vegetables right after they were picked, you would still have to eat them in extremely large amounts in order to get all the necessary vitamins vital for vitality. This is likely another one of the major contributors to the obesity problem and health problems we are experiencing in America today.

While the government recommends that you get a minimum amount of a variety of vitamins and minerals each day through fruits and vegetables, even those are woefully less than what your body really needs to work properly. In fact, you can do all the right things for your health, such as eating low-carb, drinking more water and exercising every single day. But if you don't add at least some vitamin supplements to the equation, you may hinder your progress towards attaining better overall health and successful weight loss. That's definitely not a good thing, is it?

You just never realize the importance vitamins are to your overall health until you try to live without them. Unfortunately, most people are extremely vitamin deficient because they are not getting enough of them in the foods they eat to allow their body to perform as well as it should. When you are livin' la vida low-carb and trying to lose weight, it is that much more important that you get the right amount of the vitamins and minerals your body needs.

With all the vitamin supplements out there, what specifically and how much are you supposed to take? Just walk into any health food store or your local pharmacy and you'll likely see an entire wall full of vitamins from A to Z for this and that and everything in between. You may be thinking, "Is it really necessary for me to take all of those vitamins? Isn't there one big catch-all vitamin I can take that will give me everything I need in one convenient daily pill?"

Well, while there are some very good multivitamins available in the marketplace today, unfortunately, most of them do not contain everything you need to adequately supplement your dietary needs. That's why you need to begin taking vitamin supplements to assist you with your weight loss and improving your overall health.

Of course, vitamins are still naturally found in the foods we eat. These vitamins help make the body do what it is supposed to do, including the crucial role of development and growth when you are young, as well as assisting the body with many basic and necessary human functions when you become an adult.

Robbing your body of these key vitamins can cause the onset of a multitude of adverse conditions, depending on which vitamin is being deprived from your system. Symptoms can include extreme fatigue, stunted growth, and blindness, just to name a few. In fact, sometimes these conditions can cause irreversible damage to various parts of your body. If taking vitamin supplements can prevent your body from breaking down like this, then why wouldn't you want to take them?!

It is important to remember that all vitamins are not the same either. Different vitamins perform a variety of functions for the body in many ways. But each of them play an integral part of what makes your body perform as it should.

Fat-soluble vitamins, such as A, D, E and K, can be stored in your fat tissue and liver to be used as needed. However, water-soluble vitamins, like Vitamin C and B vitamins, work exclusively in the blood and any excess is excreted when you go to the restroom. These are the vitamins that give your urine that bright yellow color in the morning (TMI!). This is simply a manifestation of the excess vitamins that could not be used by the body. But if you fail to get enough vitamins in your system, you are making yourself vulnerable to certain diseases and illnesses that are otherwise preventable with proper vitamin supplementation.

Serious health complications such as heart attack and heart disease, high cholesterol, stroke, hardening of the arteries, mental illness, bad blood circulation, damaged blood vessels, the onset of Type II diabetes, Alzheimer's disease, cancer and even death can occur without adequate vitamin intake. The body is a delicate vessel God created with specific nutritional needs to prevent these debilitating conditions from occurring.

Some positive aspects of taking vitamins, besides helping to prevent all of the diseases mentioned above, include better skin and nails, improved vision, increased energy and stamina, bowel regularity, stronger bones, lower cholesterol, lower blood pressure, and much, much more.

It's amazing how just a little bit of effort on your part to make sure you are getting the vitamins you need can make such an enormous impact on your overall health. Taking these few minor preventative actions now will keep you healthy for many years to come and stave off any major health conditions as you progress towards the twilight of your life on earth.

Are you still not convinced you need to be taking vitamin supplements while you are livin' la vida low-carb? Keep reading and you'll see why it is not only highly recommended, but absolutely necessary for your health.

Vitamin supplements take up the slack when the foods you eat fall short of providing your body what it needs. Some people think they are depriving themselves of valuable vitamin-rich foods when they are on a low-carb lifestyle because they cannot eat certain fruits and vegetables. I think we have already firmly established that today's foods have a lot less nutrients then they used to. But for the sake of this discussion, let's assume that eating fruits and vegetables will give you an adequate amount of vitamins and minerals for your body.

While you are on the first two weeks of Induction when you restrict yourself to only 20g carbs per day, you are probably not going to be able to eat as many vitamin-rich foods as you would like. This sounds like it could be detrimental to the cause of getting adequate nutrition, doesn't it?

However, think about this for a moment. What was the quality of your food intake like prior to starting a low-carb lifestyle? Were you really getting all the essential vitamins and minerals your body needs on that eating plan consisting of potato chips, sweets and sodas?

If you are like I was before I started livin' la vida low-carb, then the answer to that question is not just "no," but a resounding "no!" Most of us got fat because we made really bad decisions about the kind of foods we put in our mouths. Let's face it, potato chips, candy bars and sugar-laced sodas aren't exactly rich in the vitamins and nutrients our bodies need, are they? Let's not fool ourselves into thinking we're suddenly eating a lot worse off than we were before we got on a low-carb program. In fact, just the opposite is true.

Furthermore, you don't have to necessarily choose foods that are low in vitamin content as you progress through the various phases of your low-carb plan. Eventually you can add back those foods that provide you with the key vitamins and minerals that your body needs. Nevertheless, I would still argue that even then you will not be getting enough of the vitamins you need on a daily basis.

Whether you are just beginning your low-carb weight loss plan or if you are well on your way to reaching your goal weight, you really need to be supplementing your eating plan with vitamins to help you remain energetic and healthy on your new way of eating. The benefit to your body from vitamin supplementation is so overwhelmingly positive, it would be foolish to just completely ignore them altogether.

Have I finally convinced you that vitamin supplements are good companions to a healthy way of living? Are you now ready to take the plunge and start adding vitamin supplements to your low-carb lifestyle?

If so, then your next question for me is probably along the lines of, "What are the key vitamins I need to be taking?" I'm so glad you asked that question and I will attempt to answer it for you now.

Let's take a closer look at each of the five key vitamins that I personally took on a daily basis during my low-carb weight loss and weight maintenance plan in alphabetical order:

1. CALCIUM

We all know that calcium is needed for good bone and teeth health. But you may not realize it also plays a vital role in muscle contractions, regulating your heartbeat, and boosting you immune system, too. We need the proper amount of calcium in our bodies to allow these benefits to make us healthier and stronger.

Calcium supplements are especially important when you are on a low-carb lifestyle because regular milk is so high in carbohydrates that it should not be a part of your low-carb plan. While you can get some of the calcium you need by drinking low-carb milk, eating cheese, and munching on green leafy vegetables, it's not a bad idea to take calcium supplements. I have taken 1200 mg of calcium supplements every single day since I started livin' la vida low-carb.

I take a calcium carbonate now, but I have also taken a calcium citrate when I was losing weight. Calcium carbonate, found in the name brand Caltrate, is the most common form of calcium on the market and needs a lot of extra stomach acid to be absorbed into the body. However, calcium citrate, such as Citrical, can be absorbed without any extra stomach acid and can even be taken on an empty stomach. Both of these were effective for me and your decision about which one to take is just a matter of preference.

There are also other forms of calcium out there you can take, but one of the two versions I mentioned above will be all you need to take to fill your calcium needs.

2. FIBER

One of the things opponents of the low-carb lifestyle like to point out is how much this way of eating can make you constipated. I guess these people have too much time on their hands that they have to come up with something so incredibly stupid and ridiculous to complain about! It's obvious these people don't want those of us who are livin' la vida low-carb to enjoy our lifestyle choice. Their jealousy about our low-carb lifestyle is so transparent (okay, I'll get off my soapbox now!).

Since I consume plenty of water each day (and so will you after reading Chapter 2, right?!) and eat fiber-rich green leafy vegetables often, constipation has never been a problem for me. But, to make sure I stay regular, I also take a daily fiber supplement, such as Fibercon. Be careful about which fiber supplement you choose, though.

Some of the liquid fiber supplements as well as several brands of flavored chewable fiber tablets can have added sugars that don't help your cause when you are following a low-carb plan. Furthermore, some of them have caused me to have extreme gastric distress when I took them (that's an uncomfortable feeling you definitely don't want to experience!). I found that taking two daily Fibercon, a bulk-forming laxative that contains the active ingredient calcium polycarbophil, worked best for me.

3. FISH OIL

Once you get over the unpleasant smell and funky aftertaste, fish oil supplements are really not that bad. They can dramatically improve your heart health and lower your cholesterol and triglycerides because they contain omega-3 fatty acids. Of course, you could eat more fish to try to get many of the same benefits of fish oil in your body. But even then most people need this important supplement to get the right amount of omega-3 fatty acids they need for their body because you cannot consume enough fish oil from eating fish alone. Plus, you run into the danger of getting too much mercury in your body if you eat large amounts of fish.

The specific fish oil supplement that I take is cod liver oil softgels, which are also supplemented with 1250 IU Vitamin A, helpful with bone, tooth, nerve, and eye health as well as 130 IU Vitamin D, aiding the body as it regulates calcium and phosphorus levels for bone health.

4. MULTIVITAMINS

We all know we need to take a daily multivitamin, but how many of us actually do it? I would venture to say not very many of us do. Whether you are trying to lose weight or just want to make sure your body is getting the proper amount of vitamins and minerals it needs, you really need to start taking a multivitamin right away. I contend that this is the single most important vitamin supplement you need to take on a daily basis to fulfill your daily vitamin requirements.

Some of the key vitamins you get in your multivitamin as well as certain foods you eat on your low-carb plan include:

Vitamin A
- Good for vision health
- Promotes healthy skin
- Found in eggs

Various B Vitamins
- They are B1, B2, B12, niacin, folic acid, biotin, and pantothenic acid
- Activates your metabolism
- Increases your energy
- Makes red blood cells

- Carries oxygen throughout your body
- Found in whole grains, fish, meats, eggs and leafy green vegetables

Vitamin C
- Maintains body tissue health in your gums and muscles
- Helps your body heal from an open wound
- Increases your immune system to fight infections
- Found in strawberries and tomatoes

Vitamin D
- Strengthens bones and teeth
- Helps your body absorb calcium
- Found in low-carb milk, fish, eggs and dairy products

Vitamin E
- Preserves tissues in your eyes and skin
- Protects your lungs from pollutants in the air
- Helps form red blood cells
- Found in whole grains, leafy green vegetables, eggs and nuts

Vitamin K
- Promotes blood clotting
- Found in leafy green vegetables, liver (yucky poo!), pork and dairy products

These and other essential vitamins are found in virtually every multivitamin on the market today. However, I have found two brands that have been especially helpful to me during my low-carb weight loss and weight maintenance program.

The first one is from One A Day and it is called CarbSmart. This multivitamin contains the key vitamins, including 2500 IU Vitamin A (Beta Carotene), 90 mg Vitamin C, 400 IU Vitamin D, 45 IU Vitamin E, 25 mcg Vitamin K, 2.2 mg Thiamin (B1), 2.5 mg Riboflavin (B2), 25 mg of Niacin, 3 mg of Vitamin B6, 400 mcg

Folic Acid, 9 mcg Vitamin B12, 450 mcg Biotin (breaks down protein, which is helpful when you are on a low-carb plan), 15 mg Pantothenic Acid, 200 mg Calcium (elemental), 154 mg Phosphorus, 100 mg Magnesium, 22.5 mg Zinc, 105 mcg Selenium, 2 mg Copper, 2 mg Manganese, 200 mcg Chronium, 75 mcg Molybdenum and 99 mg Potassium

The second one is from Centrum and it is called Carb Assist. This multivitamin contains the key vitamins, including 3500 IU Vitamin A (29% as Beta Carotene), 120 mg Vitamin C, 400 IU Vitamin D, 60 IU Vitamin E, 25 mcg Vitamin K, 4.5 mg of Thiamin (B1), 5.1 mg of Riboflavin (B2), 40 mg Niacin, 6 mg Vitamin B6, 400 mcg Folic Acid, 18 mcg Vitamin B12, 40 mcg Biotin, 10 mg Pantothenic Acid, 100 mg Calcium, 48 mg Phosphorus, 150 mcg Iodine, 40 mg Magnesium, 15 mg Zinc, 70 mcg Selenium, 2 mg Copper, 4 mg Manganese, 120 mcg Chronium, 78 mcg Molybdenum, 72 mg Chloride, 80 mg Potassium, 50 mg Ginseng Root, 60 mg Gingko Biloba Leaf, 60 mcg Boron, 5 mcg Nickel, 4 mg Silicon, 10 mcg Tin and 10 mcg Vanadium.

You can decide for yourself which one you prefer to take. Both have worked equally well for me both during and after my weight loss.

5. POTASSIUM

Let me warn you now just in case you haven't heard, but you may experience some pretty excruciating leg cramps when you first start on a low-carb lifestyle primarily because of the lack of potassium in the foods you consume. Some people experience a very strong diuretic effect when they first begin their low-carb program. This will cause them to sweat a lot and deplete their body of potassium. That is why this supplement is so essential. Bananas are an excellent source of potassium, but are restricted from your eating plan when you are livin' la vida low-carb because of their high sugar content (29g carbs for just one banana!).

My remedy for this deficiency has been to take a potassium supplement or eat avocados, sardines, nuts, and almonds that all contain good amounts of potassium. The minimal amount of potassium in your multivitamin is not nearly enough to completely prevent you from having leg cramps. Therefore, you'll need to take about 300 mg of potassium each day to keep the leg cramps at bay. They are oh so very painful when you get them, but hang in there because they eventually subside once you start getting enough potassium in your system.

As far as vitamins go, that's it. Those are the vitamins that I took since I started livin' la vida low-carb. Of course, there are other vitamins you may choose to take as well. However, most of these other vitamins are found in adequate doses in your multivitamin. Consult with a certified nutritionist or your doctor about which vitamins you need to take for optimum results for your specific dietary needs.

As you can see, vitamins really are vital for vitality!

KEY POINTS TO REMEMBER FROM CHAPTER 4:

- You can't get enough vitamins from foods alone

- Vitamins protect you against illness and disease

- Get the right amount of key vitamins to help your body function properly

- Your overall health will improve when you take vitamin supplements

- Take a calcium supplement for strong bones and teeth

- Take a fiber supplement to maintain regular bowel movements

- Take a fish oil supplement to get omega-3 fatty acids for heart health

- Take a multivitamin to get essential vitamins and minerals

- Take potassium supplements to prevent leg cramps on low-carb

- Consult with your doctor or nutritionist about what vitamins to take

Chapter 5
Motivation That Moves You

One of the most intriguing questions I am most often asked by people since losing 180 pounds and keeping it off on the low-carb lifestyle is, "What motivated you to get started on the low-carb lifestyle and actually stick with it?" Now that's an excellent question for someone to ask who is contemplating making a similar radical change in their own life and I will do my best to reveal my answer to that question in this chapter.

Keep in mind that my motivation for beginning and staying on a low-carb lifestyle may not necessarily be the same as yours. At the same time, you may see a lot of similarities to your own life in the stories I'll share with you. If nothing else, I hope this chapter about what motivated me to begin a low-carb lifestyle will light a fire within you to do it, too.

I am encouraged by the fact that you purchased my book because it tells me you are serious about making this commitment to begin a low-carb lifestyle. It is my prayer that you have already been inspired and motivated by my personal experiences of being successful on this way of eating.

Real-life examples of people who have been successful on the low-carb lifestyle can certainly motivate you to do it for yourself. That was one of the primary reasons why I wrote this book so it would encourage others who were where I was not that long ago to make the decision to begin a low-carb weight loss plan for the sake of losing those extra pounds they've been carrying around as well as restoring their overall health.

There are two men that I know personally who lost a lot of weight on the low-carb lifestyle in recent years. Neither one of them probably even realize the enormous impact their personal success stories had on me to get me motivated about making this happen for myself.

The first one is a man by the name of Keith Jackson. Keith and I were in the same high school class at Bolivar Central High School in Bolivar, TN in the late 1980s. Like me, Keith was overweight when he was in high school. But I could not believe my eyes at my 10-year high school class reunion in 1999 when somebody told me that skinny man with the goatee I inquired about was none other than Keith Jackson himself. I remember staring at him for what seemed like an eternity completely mesmerized by his incredibly radical change in appearance. This former chubby classmate of mine had dropped a considerable amount of his weight and restored his health by implementing a low-carb program. Although I was still skeptical of the low-carb lifestyle at the time, I never forgot the dramatic change in Keith's physical appearance.

The other man that motivated me about beginning a low-carb lifestyle was my half-brother Nathan Moore. "Nat," as we called him growing up, was a memorable fat kid whose pants hung so far below his belly that you could see his stomach hanging out and the crack of his butt sticking out the back. He was the quintessential slob. He really didn't care about what he looked like as long as he could eat his cheeseburgers and french fries at our dad's restaurants. But as Nathan grew older, he became more and more aware of his bad eating habits and turned to low-carb to get thin in his late teens.

To this day, Nathan has successfully kept his weight off for good thanks to livin' la vida low-carb. I don't know whether Keith has actually kept his weight off or not (I may find out at my 20-year high school class reunion in 2009), but I often thought about both of their personal triumphs when I decided to start my own low-carb lifestyle. Their example that it could be done convinced me that this was something that I could do, too.

Believe it or not, I didn't purposely try to search out any other low-carb success stories in books or on the Internet to motivate me to get started on my own low-carb weight loss plan. Actually, the few times I casually looked for a low-carb success story book at my local Barnes & Noble store or at Amazon.com, I couldn't find one anywhere. That's yet another reason I decided to write this book so people could read about a real life example of someone who did it the low-carb way and lived to tell about it!

Although I have always considered myself to be a self-motivator who can stick with virtually anything I set my mind to doing (the fact that I was able to write this entire book from start to finish is yet another example of this characteristic God has bestowed on me!), I guess I didn't think about looking to the example of those who have gone before me and reached their goals on the low-carb lifestyle. However, if that is something that gets you going, then there are plenty of places online for you to see other people's success stories. All you need to do is a quick Google search on the keywords "low-carb success stories" and you'll find plenty of inspiration and motivation to last you a lifetime.

It's hard for me personally to give up on something when I become thoroughly passionate about it. The challenge of doing something that seems too impossible to come to fruition or if others are skeptical about whether or not I can overcome an obstacle is an enormous motivating factor for me. If you can get my competitive juices flowing, then you had better look out because I can't be stopped until I get it done.

That's probably why I was so successful losing weight on a low-fat diet in 1999. My own personal will to make it happen probably accounted for the overwhelming majority of my weight loss. My downfall with that ultimately was the fact that I didn't have the perseverance to keep it off. I'll get into that topic in Chapter 9 because it is just as important to endure even after the initial burst of motivation begins to wane in your weight loss journey.

Some have hypothesized that I must have had some strong "willpower" or "determination" to motivate me to accomplish such an enormous amount of weight loss on the low-carb lifestyle. I laugh when I hear people say this to me because I really don't consider myself to be someone with any willpower whatsoever, especially when it comes to food.

In all honesty, I would certainly describe myself as strong-willed and determined, but I used to be extremely vulnerable when it came to foods that I really should not have been eating, namely sugary sweets and pasta. These foods acted as my own personal Kryptonite! But the change that happened in me regarding these and other high-carb foods is a miracle from God to say the least. I credit my faith in the Lord God Almighty for helping me overcome these food addictions for good when I started livin' la vida low-carb.

Incredibly, some of those same foods that used to excite me and make me want to eat gobs and gobs of them now make me want to hurl just looking at them (remember my macaroni and cheese story?)! If that's not a miracle, then I don't know what is! Perhaps hearing my story of triumph over these foods will help motivate you to continue on with your low-carb lifestyle even when temptation lurks around the corner (and it will!).

Despite my best efforts, dealing with my weight problem had always been a big struggle for me. There were some days I would just look in the mirror and wonder how in the world I ever got to the point in my life where I would allow myself to weigh over 400 pounds! I am thoroughly convinced that when you allow yourself to get that big and continue eating like there will be no consequences to your weight or health, then you have already given up on yourself. This is an extremely dangerous place to allow yourself to get.

Sadly, that is a perfect description of where my only full-blooded brother is. Kevin is just four years my senior and has struggled with weight problems his entire life just like I used to. Weighing at least 400 pounds himself, he suffered a series of nearly fatal heart attacks in the late 1990s that could have killed him because of his extreme weight problem.

By the grace and mercy of God, Kevin is still alive today, but with limited ability to live the life he once dreamed about. He depends on a defibrillator and heavy medication to maintain the flailing health of his heart. Unfortunately, he remains morbidly obese because he apparently sees no hope for the future regarding his health and weight.

Seeing the life that Kevin has had to live since that horrifying experience was one of the things that inspired me to do something about my own weight problem. In fact, he was my original motivation for trying to lose weight in 1999 when I lost 170 pounds on a low-fat diet. I remember losing all that weight and thinking I had finally done something to prevent what happened to my brother from happening to me. Yet the failure of the low-fat diet to produce long-term weight maintenance did me in and the weight poured back on like gangbusters. But I never, ever forgot about Kevin's health situation. When I started my low-carb plan in 2004, I vowed to stick with it and remain motivated so I could be an example for him to see someday.

I was fortunate enough to visit my brother in Pensacola, Florida over the Christmas holidays in 2004 and he was utterly amazed by my 180-pound weight loss. Now, I pray that the small success I have been blessed to achieve through this experience will spur him to improve his health through weight loss as soon as possible. I love you Kevin, and want you to be motivated to do this as much as I was!

For the tens of millions of Americans who have constantly tried and failed to lose weight over their entire lives, it is easy to think there's no use even trying to lose weight yet again because it will just keep coming back over and over again. This defeatist mentality only serves to rob you of the motivation you will need to get started and finally do something about it that really works.

Whatever you do, don't allow past diet failures to cause you to give up now. This is a new day for you and you're going to do it this time around! Believe it for yourself! Whenever you feel like giving up, think about this man you know who used to weigh 410 pounds and remember that he's never going to go back there ever again. Yippee!

There's a dirty little secret that low-fat supporters don't want you to know about regarding their preferred method of weight loss. While it very well may work for people who don't mind being hungry all the time and eating nasty-tasting foods that are supposedly "healthy" for them, the low-fat diets don't necessarily work for everyone who desires to find a permanent solution to their weight problem. I know this is true because I tried, lost some weight, but then failed to keep it off so many times on a low-fat diet that I lost count. That's why livin' la vida low-carb was so attractive to me and motivated me to give it a chance. After all, what did I have to lose (well, as it turns out, 180 pounds!)?

Let me warn you now about something that is entirely unique to the low-carb lifestyle so you can be ready for it. Even if you consider yourself a strong person mentally and aren't your own worst enemy when it comes to beating yourself up about weight loss, don't worry because there will be plenty of people out there who will do it for you! Many good-intentioned people will actively seek to drain you of every drop of motivation you may currently have and will try to completely discourage you from going through with your low-carb lifestyle.

It is as if some people in this world think it is their mission in life to point out anything and everything that is wrong with the low-carb program and to ignorantly criticize it in front of people who are sincerely trying to lose weight and get healthy. They want to prevent you from following this real alternative to the failed low-fat/low-calorie/portion-controlled diets that have plagued us for generations. I know many of these people, including your friends and family, undoubtedly mean well, but they have absolutely no idea what they are talking about in regards to the low-carb lifestyle.

Therefore, as a public service to you, let me share with you just a small sample of the many objections you will most certainly face when you are livin' la vida low-carb. Amazingly, even after my 180-pound weight loss following a low-carb program, can you believe I still hear many of these same arguments from time to time?! What more can I do to prove to these people that low-carb really works?

I have learned that you just have to laugh when you hear these same excuses over and over again for not doing a low-carb lifestyle. I challenge you to use these excuses people give you as opportunities to educate them further about why you have chosen this way of eating as your preferred weight loss and weight maintenance program.

Be prepared to encounter some variation of the following arguments people will use against you to demotivate you when you are attempting to follow a low-carb lifestyle:

TOP TEN ARGUMENTS AGAINST DOING LOW-CARB

1. **It's not healthy.**

This is complete and utter hogwash! The low-carb lifestyle has been and is continuing to be supported by plenty of research that confirms it is a healthy alternative to the low-fat/low-calorie diets. Not only is eating the low-carb way healthy, but it is a lot more satisfying and enjoyable than the rabbit food you are forced to eat when you are on those other diets. Do you want to know what is unhealthy? The most unhealthy thing you can do is walk around as an overweight or obese person and do nothing about it! That's just about as unhealthy as you can ever be! But thanks to livin' la vida low-carb, that problem is solved quickly and permanently.

2. **It's dangerous.**

This is intellectually dishonest and has never been fully explained by anyone who has ever said it. Low-fat advocates like to warn people about the higher fat content found in certain low-carb foods. But anyone who does even a little bit of research on low-carb programs will find that fat is not only good for you, but absolutely necessary to bring about weight loss and improvements in your cholesterol, triglycerides and overall health. If you don't understand how low-carb works, then how can you label it dangerous? Interestingly, a study conducted by Washington University at St. Louis in May 2005 found that not eating enough fat in your diet will actually cause you to gain weight! Now there's some scientific evidence that proves low-fat is the real dangerous diet.

3. **It's only for the short-term.**

Says who? I was on a low-carb program for about a year during my 180-pound weight loss, but I have remained on my carb-conscious eating plan to maintain the weight loss ever since. If it's just for the short-term, then how are you supposed to eat over the long-term? And don't tell me I need to go back to eating a low-fat diet, either! Been there, done that, and couldn't keep the weight off. I think I'll be sticking with my low-carb lifestyle, thank you very much!

4. **It's just a "fad" diet.**

Hmmm, the low-carb approach is a "fad" diet, eh? What is the definition of a fad? Isn't it something that burns hot for a short amount of time and then dies off quickly? Well, the low-carb lifestyle has been around prominently in America since the early 1970's and has continued to grow by leaps and bounds in popularity more that three decades later as people find it to be an excellent alternative to low-fat diets. In fact, with an estimated 45 million Americans on some version of the low-carb lifestyle in 2005 according to an Opinion Dynamics Corp survey, that makes it 50 percent more popular than the #1 show on television, *American Idol*! Yep, livin' la vida low-carb sure sounds like a fad to me! Where do these people come up with this stuff?!

5. **You'll damage your kidneys.**

Research supports the fact that people on a low-carb way of eating experience normalized kidney function if their kidneys were healthy prior to beginning the program. For me personally, since I started livin' la vida low-carb and increasing my water intake, my kidneys have been doing just fine. I have not personally had any adverse effect on my kidneys whatsoever since I have been on my low-carb lifestyle. Again, there is no medical evidence that shows you will incur damage to your kidneys as a result of following a low-carb way of eating. Now leave my kidneys alone or I'll send them over to beat up on your liver!

6. **Ketosis causes you to have bad breath.**

There's an easy answer this this: pop a sugar-free breath mint! Getting your body into fat-burning mode is the underlying premise behind the low-carb lifestyle. Ketosis is a natural bodily function that occurs when your body is ridding itself of stored fat and should not be avoided just so you can keep your breath smelling pretty. Think about all that weight you're gonna be shedding instead of worrying about how funky your breath may smell! Avoiding a low-carb lifestyle just because ketosis makes your breath stink is about as ridiculous as avoiding exercise because it makes your underarms stink!

7. **You can't exercise on a low-carb plan.**

Speaking of exercise, I have already addressed this subject in a previous chapter, but let's just say you won't have any trouble getting the exercise you need on your low-carb lifestyle. I get a minimum of 60 minutes or more combined of both cardiovascular and weight lifting exercise every single day! Anyone who tells you not to exercise while on a low-carb plan must want you to fail. Exercise is not an option, but rather a necessity when you are livin' la vida low-carb.

8. **All you eat is meat.**

Why do people automatically assume people only eat meat when they are eating the low-carb way?! There are so many non-animal foods available for people desiring to do this lifestyle, such as green vegetables, nuts, cheese, eggs, whole wheat breads, berries and more. The selection of foods besides meat when you follow the low-carb approach is endless. A complete list of acceptable low-carb foods can be found in just about every low-carb book out there today. But tell me something? Who wouldn't want to chow down on some tender delicious meals consisting of steak, chicken, fish, or bacon every once in a while? Food on a weight loss program never tasted so good! This is the life, man!

9. **If you eat all that fat, then you'll clog your arteries.**

Oh, I just love this one because it was one I used to tell people before I educated myself further about the benefits of eating low-carb. Fat is not the great evil when it comes to losing weight. Although that's the lie we've been fed our entire lives, it's just not true. Research shows that eating fat combined with a low-carb approach does not increase cardiovascular risk factors, but actually improves your overall heart health. On a low-carb lifestyle, fat is absolutely essential to help the body lose weight and feel satisfied. It's time for people to get over their fat-phobia and learn the rest of the story regarding this important element in low-carb living. Say it with me now, "fat is good for you." You might need to ask people to repeat that phrase at least a couple hundred times before the truth of that statement begins to sink into their thick indoctrinated skulls!

10. **You can't eat fruits and vegetables.**

Again, this is a big, fat lie. When you are just starting off on your low-carb lifestyle, especially on the first two weeks of Induction, you are restricting yourself on a lot of different kinds of foods. However, you quickly begin adding back tasty fruits and vegetables such as lettuce, green beans, cauliflower, strawberries, blueberries and more after the first two weeks of your low-carb plan. When you reach lifetime maintenance, you can add back a whole lot more of the fruits and vegetables you love. But a lot of people don't even realize the extremely high sugar content of supposedly "healthy" foods such as bananas, carrots, apples and oranges. You are much better off not eating any of these foods in excess, even if they are so-called "healthy" fruits and vegetables. The sugar content found in them will destroy your low-carb plan and can cause you to gain weight if you eat too many of them.

I'm sure you will hear plenty of other arguments to try to discourage you from continuing on with your low-carb program. But preparing yourself now for these oft-repeated phrases will hopefully convince you even more that livin' la vida low-carb is right for you. Don't let these people convince you otherwise. Low-carb really works despite its naysayers!

When I think about my own personal motivation for losing weight, I recollect on a series of events and memories in the months leading up to starting the low-carb lifestyle that I won't soon forget. Some of these stories may sound vaguely familiar to you if you have struggled with being overweight or obese for any length of time. I pray these stories from my own life about what motivated me to get serious about losing weight will motivate you, too.

When you think about being a big person, it's hard not to hate flying on an airplane. It has nothing to do with being scared of flying or being worried about anything bad happening. Frankly, it's the fact that airplane seats seem to be made for skinny people. I am thoroughly convinced this is a conspiracy against obese people. Just kidding!

Do you know how unbelievably embarrassing it is to have to ask the stewardess for a seat belt extension just so you can buckle your seat belt? Or how about the humbling experience of having your butt get stuck in that seat as it squeezes your body like a can of sardines? The same goes for movie theater seats and tight booths at restaurants. It may be funny to some people, but when you are overweight and feel helpless, it is no laughing matter.

How about the seemingly simple, everyday task of getting in and out of your car? Sounds easy enough, doesn't it? But when you are a heavy person, even this menial task can be a challenge. I can remember having to slowly ease my way in and out of my Ford Escort so I wouldn't hurt myself before I lost weight. I would almost always get a painful hip pointer every time I needed to drive because of the way I had to force myself in and pry myself out of my car. This process of entering and exiting my vehicle would sometimes take several minutes since I had gotten way too big for my car. Does this remind you of anyone you know?

My protruding belly would literally hug the front of the steering wheel like a pair of tight Spandex pants and my thighs would push up on the bottom of the steering wheel in the most uncomfortable manner. In fact, I probably could have steered my car just using my stomach all by itself if I wanted to! This daily chore of getting in and out of the car probably looked like a hilarious comedy skit to my neighbors who may have been watching, but it was an unfortunate part of my daily life that I was not happy about one bit. The obvious frustration I was feeling about this scenario was my first inkling of motivation beginning to develop inside me of me.

I also remember the time I tried to climb a rock wall during my church's annual Fall Festival event several months before starting my low-carb weight loss plan. I had watched a few other adult men in the church get strapped to the harness and climb that rock wall like Spiderman. I didn't even think twice about not trying to do it because it didn't look like it would be that difficult. Boy was I in for a surprise!

When it was my turn to do it, I put the tight fitting cord around my legs and waist so it would protect me from falling. Then I proceeded to attempt my first step. Slip, umpf. Not to be intimidated by this rock wall, I tried again to take a single step. Slip, umpf ... again.

I turned around and looked at everyone staring at me and cheering me on to do it. It was at that moment I realized I probably wouldn't be climbing the rock wall that day. Even still, I'm hardheaded and tried one more time to climb up that wall. This time though, not only did I "slip" and "umpf," but I also twisted my ankle. Thankfully I merely sprained my ankle, but it was at this point that I had yet another vivid memory playing in my head of just how big I had allowed myself to get. As a result, my motivation to do something about my weight problem began to build within me even more.

Then there's the matter-of-fact comment I got from this short, pudgy little 7th grade boy at the local junior high school just before beginning my low-carb plan. I was his substitute teacher for the day and standing in front of the class explaining the English assignment his class would be working on that day. I was walking around the front of the room and providing instruction to several students about their classwork.

As I approached the chalkboard to begin writing something about the assignment on it, I heard four harrowing words that still ring loudly in my head to this day.

"Mr. Moore is fffffat!" he exclaimed.

Of course, as soon as he said that, the entire class of 13-year-old kids burst into laughter and so did I, although I am sure my laughter was more in response to the shock of the student's comment and how sad but true it really was. There was no doubt about that fact whatsoever in anybody's mind that day.

We've all heard the insults and jokes about our weight, haven't we? You can allow comments like that to either motivate or discourage you. But no matter how insensitive and biting such impromptu comments can be, you can decide for yourself to allow those words to motivate you to lose weight for good. That is exactly what I did. Even if that little runt who said I was "fffffat" needed to lose about 30 pounds himself! Hee hee!

As painful as all these incidents have been on me psychologically, nothing irked me more than the time I dropped a piece of chalk on the floor when I was substitute teaching in a local elementary school. I was wearing some pants that day that weren't particularly loose, but I didn't think they were very tight either. Nevertheless, when I bent over to pick up the chalk, I heard the most horrifying sound an overweight person will ever hear -- rrrriiiiipppp!!! I literally tore my pants right down the middle of my crotch and up the back of my pants. Do you realize how hard it was to teach those kids for the rest of the day?! I actually had to remain seated for most of the day and quickly exited when the school day was over so I could go home and change my pants. Sound familiar, anyone?

Stories like this abound when you carry around a lot of extra weight. Thinking back in your own life, you can probably come up with a lot more stories just like these from your recent past that you can use to motivate yourself to get serious about your weight loss. When it came time for me to do that for myself, these were the experiences that helped motivate me to do it!

The people in our lives can also be an amazing motivating factor that will help you to lose weight, too. Besides Keith and Nathan, who I have previously mentioned, my wife, Christine, and many others were instrumental in giving me the support system I needed to get started on this weight loss and to keep me going. I'll talk further about how important it is to have a support system around you in a Chapter 8 because it is an incredible motivating factor during your weight loss and weight maintenance experience.

Besides stories like the ones I mentioned above and people in your life, another thing that can motivate you to begin a permanent weight loss strategy is the condition of your health. I have been fortunate enough to have had near-perfect health throughout my entire life without any major conditions or ailments. I've never had to endure anything medically serious despite being obese for most of my childhood and adult life.

After I started my low-carb lifestyle, though, I went to my doctor to get a physical checkup to see how my health was doing. There is nothing I could have done to prepare myself for the message I was about to hear from my doctor.

Three months after I began livin' la vida low-carb and had already lost about 80 pounds, I went to see my family doctor to let him know about my weight loss progress and to get a full health examination. Little did I know he would have some good news and some bad news to tell me.

The bad news was that I had developed high blood pressure, which had gotten as high as 175/98, and high total cholesterol, which was around 278 as a result of my obesity prior to beginning the low-carb lifestyle. While those numbers really didn't surprise me too much considering how big I had gotten before losing weight, it was what he said to me next that took my breath away and nearly caused me to pass out.

He looked right at me with a somber face and bluntly stated, "Jimmy, had you not started losing weight a few months ago, you were right on the verge of suffering what would have likely been a fatal heart attack!" This was supposed to be the good news?!

Yikes! I don't care how depressed you are about your weight problem, a statement like that from your doctor will most certainly wake you up and motivate even the weakest person to do what you have to do to improve your health. That's exactly what I set out to do from that day forward. I think more doctors need to be honest with their patients and warn them of the harmful effects obesity can and will have on their health.

By the grace of God I was able to dig myself out of that deep hole I had dug for myself that would have certainly led me to an early grave. Anytime I ever felt like I couldn't do this anymore, I thought about the words my doctor told me that day. It has worked every time to motivate me to keep on keeping on! The gratifying part is now I know I have added many years to my life because of the lifestyle changes I have made.

Even if your health is not in imminent danger, you must know how unhealthy it is to carry around more weight than you need. While you may not have any obvious health problems that you know about right now, you are certainly endangering yourself by not addressing your obesity problem immediately. Think about that for just a moment and allow it to motivate you like you've never been motivated before.

Once I got motivated to start my own low-carb plan, there were several things I did right away that helped keep me motivated.

On the first week I started livin' la vida low-carb, my wife and I were in the local mall and we went to a popular clothing chain store (not a big and tall store!) where we had a gift card. While we were shopping, I suddenly got a bright idea and told my wife that I would be going to the men's section to look around. About five minutes later, I returned carrying a brand new pair of khaki slacks.

Baffled by the garment I was holding in my hands, my wife asked me what size the pants were. I proudly told her they were 42/32. Keep in mind that this was just my first week on my low-carb program and my waist size at that time was 62/32. My wife looked at me like I was crazy for buying a pair of pants 20 inches smaller than what I was wearing at the time. But I envisioned a plan for these "goal pants." They would give me something to look forward to when I got down to the weight I needed to be.

When we got home, I hung those pants up in a prominent place in my bedroom as a constant reminder of where I needed to be when I reached my goal weight someday. From time to time during my weight loss, I would try these "goal pants" on just to see how they would fit! As the months progressed, I eventually got past getting just one of my legs in the pants. Amazingly, this crazy "goal pants" idea worked to perfection and I was finally able to fit into them after ten months of livin' la vida low-carb. Today, those "goal pants" are now loose on me. Oh the spoils of eight loss success! You should be confident that the same success will happen for you, too!

Of course, I also had something else rather unusual to motivate me to lose weight -- that radio contest! While I don't expect you to enter any kind of contest to give you the motivation to lose weight, it certainly didn't hurt my cause. I'm very competitive as I stated earlier and not the kind of person to back down form a challenge. It is interesting that the radio contest motivated me as much as it did and yet every other contestant dropped out before the final weigh-in. This just goes to show you that incentive alone does not necessarily give you the motivation, but merely enables you to have some sort of reward to strive for. If you want to lose weight bad enough, then you'll get it done regardless of any prize you could win. The biggest prize you'll win is a thin and healthy body!

Nevertheless, NBC's hit reality show "The Biggest Loser" is a perfect example that money can be a strong incentive to get people to lose weight. When the first season of this show aired in the summer of 2004, I had already lost a majority of my weight. But it was still extremely motivating for me to watch those contestants as they overcame their own personal struggles to lose a lot of weight just like I had. Although it would have been fun to be on that show, I don't know if I could have shown my "man boobs" (as one of the contestants called them) on national television. Watching television shows like this one can certainly help get you motivated.

People always want to know what motivated me to endure in my weight loss when it would stall. What I tell people is you need to keep doing the plan as if it's working like a charm even when you're not losing pounds. If the scale is demotivating you from continuing on with your low-carb program, then put it away for a few weeks. My motto during my weight loss was that nothing was going to sidetrack or discourage me from doing this. Once you get this kind of motivation inside of you, success is not far behind. The perseverance that keeps you going over the long-term will be discussed further in Chapter 9.

There you have it. That's just a little bit of what motivated me to get started and to stay committed to this low-carb lifestyle no matter what. What about you? Have you thought about your own life experiences that will help motivate you? I encourage you to think about it for yourself and bring these stories to the forefront of your mind to get serious about your weight problem. Allow yourself to make this mindset change permanent so you never allow yourself to get back to where you were before you became skinny (it's still hard for me to get used to hearing people describe me using that word!). Tell that fat person to pack up and move out because the lean, mean, sexy machine that lives inside of you is just begging to be let loose. It's time to let him or her out!

One final bit of motivation you can lean on is the fact that you now know someone who used to be in your shoes and was able to lose 180 pounds following a low-carb lifestyle. I am convinced that God allowed me to lose all of that weight so I could help people who need motivation and encouragement as they begin livin' la vida low-carb for themselves.

That's why I decided to write this book and to create my blog called "Livin' La Vida Low-Carb" (livinlavidalocarb.blogspot.com). My blog provides up-to-date information about the low-carb lifestyle, lots of before and after pictures, the latest news and information about the low-carb lifestyle, as well as poignant commentary that attempts to combat the lies that permeate throughout the media regarding the healthy low-carb way of eating. You can also e-mail me with questions or comments about low-carb at livinlowcarbman@charter.net. I respond to every e-mail I receive and would be honored to hear from you with any feedback you have about this book or anything to do with livin' la vida low-carb.

Whatever it takes to get yourself motivated, you need to find it within yourself to do it. You can do this! I know you can because I already have! Finding the motivation that moves you is now up to you.

KEY POINTS TO REMEMBER FROM CHAPTER 5:

- Find real-life examples of low-carb success stories to motivate you

- Pray that God will strengthen you to overcome your addiction to food

- Don't allow yourself to give up hope for permanent weight loss

- Be prepared for people who will try to discourage you from starting your low-carb plan

- Allow my stories about what motivated me to encourage you

- Think about your own stories and let them motivate you

- Let the present or future condition of your health motivate you

- Buy a pair of "goal pants" that you would like to fit in someday

- Watch or participate in weight loss contests

- Visit low-carb blogs and Internet web sites often to stay motivated

Chapter 6
Sugar Is Rat Poison

(Singing out loud) "Sugar pie, honey bun... I can't help myself..."

Oh, hi there! I got so caught up in thinking about the subject matter of this chapter that a whole buncha songs just started playing in my head all of a sudden that express our deep infatuation with that sweetest of all ingredients we put in our mouths -- sugar!

We Americans sure do love eating sugar and lots of it, too!

(Singing again) "Sugar, awww, honey honey..."

Did you know the average American consumes in excess of 150 pounds of sugar each year? WOW, that's a lotta sugar! If you do the math and average that out per week, that means people in this country eat nearly 3 pounds of sugar every single week! Looks like we get to have our sugar and eat it, too!

What's really scary is that some people are getting a whole lot more than a mere 3 pounds a week to make up for those of us who either don't eat sugar (because we are on the low-carb lifestyle) or can't eat sugar (because they're diabetic or have some other medical condition that prohibits them from having sugar). Can you imagine eating that much sugar day after day, week after week, year after year?!

Actually, yes I can imagine it because I was once one of those who probably ate enough sugar for ten people prior to my change to the low-carb lifestyle.

Before I started livin' la vida low-carb, I was arguably the biggest sugarholic you would have ever met in your entire life! Besides drinking my 200 ounces of sugary sodas a day totaling in excess of 500 grams of pure unadulterated sugar, I also stuffed my face with large quantities of Little Debbie snack cakes (Oatmeal Cookie, Fudge Rounds, Nutty Bar, and Swiss Miss Rolls come to mind as my favorites) and all kinds of candy bars and other sugary snacks. It really didn't matter to me what kind of sugar product it was. As long as it was sweet and loaded with sugar, then I was probably going to put it in my mouth and not even think twice about it.

My real weakness was doughnuts. I could never eat just one doughnut if somebody brought some to work or to my Sunday School class at church. I'd usually start with at least three or four of them and sometimes eat as many as eight! All the while, I was washing it down with even more sugar in the sodas I was drinking with them.

Believe it or not, sometimes I would even start eating sweets for no apparent reason at all just because I was bored or wasn't feeling good at the time. Now how lame is that?!

(Spontaneous singing yet again) "Pour some sugar on me..."

Okay, I'll stop with the singing now. But I think you get the point. Sugar is prevalent throughout our society and has been deemed socially acceptable by most everyone. There is no massive outcry from the public against sugar because most people don't view it as anything they need to be worried about.

Do you want an example of how deeply ingrained sugar has become in our culture? Think for a moment about some of the terms of endearment you use for the ones you love. Have you ever called your significant other "Sugar," "Sweetie," or "Honey?" These positive associations we make in our relationships convey a subliminal message that sugar is something to be cherished and loved.

Furthermore, sugar can be found in virtually every food product you see on the grocery store shelves today, including some of the so-called diet foods. I'll get into that touchy subject a little bit later in this chapter.

Thinking back now on my old eating habits, I can recall my daily routine of stopping at the corner convenience store on the way to work and grabbing a 64-ounce cup of high fructose corn syrup-sweetened soda along with some oversized sugar-laced soft chocolate chip cookies and a big cinnamon bun dripping with even more sugar! What's really scary to me now is the fact that I would eat that entire entourage of sugary snacks completely and wash it down before I even got to work!

Is it any wonder how I became the 410-pound poster child for morbid obesity? It literally disgusts me to even think about all of those bad eating habits I had before I started livin' la vida low-carb. What was I thinking?!?! Thank the good Lord those days are just a fading memory now that will forever be in the past.

Does this remind you of anyone you know? Maybe it's that person in the mirror staring back at you with a desperate look of hopelessness because of a very real weight problem. If so, then take heart because I am living proof that you can get out of this deep pit of despair and overcome your addiction to sugar.

While most of the media attention seems to focus on the role of fat on the obesity problem we have in the United States, I think it is time we take a closer look at the lasting impact that sugar has played in causing people to pack on the pounds. There is a lot more harm that comes from this sweet white granular substance than you might expect. Add to that the equally harmful high fructose corn syrup and you've got a 1-2 punch of ingredients that will cause you to quickly gain a whole lot of weight.

Is sugar your ultimate weakness when it comes to the low-carb lifestyle? Do you really believe there is no way you could ever possibly give up this sweet delicacy that has made so many of your favorite foods taste so good over the years? If so, then you definitely need to keep reading this chapter to find out how I broke my sugar addiction once and for all so that now even just the thought of eating sugar makes me sick to my stomach.

As a former kindred spirt regarding the perceived need for sugar in my life, I have some very good news for you. If you take what I have to say in the following pages regarding sugar seriously, then it will make you completely despise anything and everything that contains sugar and you will absolutely avoid sugary foods for the rest of your life. Really, you will. Impossible, you say? Keep reading.

When I first started my low-carb lifestyle, I created this mantra that I could literally repeat to myself out loud to help me overcome my desire for anything that contains sugar in it. There's nothing particularly special about this phrase and it's not the end-all magic words for anyone wanting to give up their sugar addiction. But it certainly helped me put things in perspective long enough for me to overcome my desire to eat sugar.

Are you ready for it? Do you want to know what this phrase is that I would constantly repeat to myself anytime I saw a food item that I knew was loaded with sugar?

Here it is: *"Sugar is rat poison!"*

That's it! That's the slogan I used to prevent myself from eating sugar! I know, I know, it's the name of this chapter so it wasn't such a big secret. But as simple and unassuming as that little four-word phrase is, it is precisely how I was able to defeat sugar's grip on me once and for all.

Saying the phrase "sugar is rat poison" can help you whenever you see a dessert that looks so incredibly delicious that you don't know how you could ever live without it. The message communicated by that phrase certainly puts things in perspective, though, don't you think? I don't care how good something looks, smells or potentially tastes, you're not going to put that food anywhere near your mouth if you treat it like it is rat poison.

What is so incredibly amazing about using this phrase is how quick and easy it is to implement. Since day one of my low-carb lifestyle, I have honestly convinced myself that eating sugar is tantamount to eating rat poison. Because of that, I have not and will not allow myself to give in to any temptation whatsoever knowing the end result would be detrimental to my health and weight loss goals. While I am still cognizant of reality and know I wouldn't actually physically die from eating sugar like I would from eating rat poison, just making this analogy and repeating it whenever I am faced with temptation for sugar turns me off to it completely.

As I was losing weight, I would often be faced with foods that I know had a lot of sugar in them. I can remember how I would immediately close my eyes and chant that familiar phrase "sugar is rat poison" over and over again in my mind to prevent me from unnecessarily splurging on the food I couldn't have which would have ruined the progress I had made on my low-carb lifestyle.

Guess what? It worked! It really did! I can confidently and honestly say that I avoided any and all sugary foods for the duration of my weight loss. Even now, I have no desire to consume any excessive sugar when I know I can live without it!

A University of California-Irvine study released in August 2005 found that creating false memories in your mind regarding certain foods can actually cause your desire for those foods to wane. That's exactly what I did by associating sugar with rat poison. I know in my experience with sugar, I can put a slice of chocolate cake right in front of my face and not be tempted any longer. While the cake certainly looks and smells good, I have absolutely no desire to eat it ever again. I don't know why or how this has happened, I just know by the grace of God it is not a point of weakness for me any longer.

Some may scoff at this "sugar is rat poison" strategy and say it's just a mind game and does nothing to help with the cravings. Perhaps. But while the psychology of it involves convincing yourself that sugar is actually rat poison even for just a split second, my experience has been that it really works if you allow yourself to earnestly believe it. Making yourself equate sugar with rat poison causes a breakthrough transformation in your mind which will lead to better eating habits being learned.

But, to be perfectly honest, comparing sugar to rat poison is not quite as far-fetched as it might initially sound. The real danger to your health that sugar poses has not been widely circulated and must be taken into consideration by anyone looking to make improvements in their weight and health.

Sugar is the substance directly responsible for causing your blood glucose levels to rise and fall. Wide variances in your blood sugar can cause you to feel irritable and tired and can usually cause you pain in various parts of your body. Additionally, just like someone who is addicted to drugs or alcohol, your body will quickly go into withdrawals and literally cause you to crave even more sugar just to satisfy the addiction. That's why you feel so run down not too long after eating a candy bar. It may give you an initial burst of energy, but you soon begin to feel sluggish and worn out.

The pain associated with the cravings for sugar explains why so many people give in and start eating sugary snacks when their energy is depleted or if they desire "comfort food" to make themselves feel better when they get depressed. While doing this to satisfy your sweet tooth might make you temporarily feel better, the symptoms of sugar withdrawal will soon return again with a vengeance and be even stronger than they were before as the vicious cycle of sugar addiction never seems to be broken. That alone should make you want to give up sugar as soon as possible!

When you are livin' la vida low-carb and attempting to completely avoid sugar in the foods you eat, the resulting experience is a marked increase in energy and bypassing all of the negative consequences associated with consuming too much sugar. Life without sugar is a place we all need to be in, but sugar addiction has a mighty stronghold on most people. It's not an easy path to take trying to beat this addiction, but it is one that is essential to being successful on your low-carb program.

You might be thinking, "I'm not addicted to sugar. I could stop eating sugar today and it would have no affect on my body whatsoever." Oh really. Then here's a challenge for you to try if you think you're not addicted to sugar. For the next 30 days, don't eat or drink anything that has sugar in it. That includes foods and beverages that contain high fructose corn syrup as well. When that month is over and you feel like you want to die, then come back and tell me that sugar isn't addictive.

I am thoroughly convinced of the fact that there is a direct link between the consumption of sugar and the obesity epidemic in the United States. Sugar-laced foods are more rapidly absorbed into the bloodstream and cause a quicker reaction to your blood sugar than those that do not have sugar in them. While there is a lot of debate about the actual causes of obesity these days, including popular theories about eating too much fat or calories, more and more people are beginning to realize the intriguing role sugar has played in making people become overweight and obese.

While some people may not have made this connection between sugar and obesity yet, most of us have known since grade school that sugar can cause damage to our teeth. Now that I'm in my early thirties, I am thoroughly convinced of this fact because I have already had four root canals in addition to having four other teeth pulled due to severe tooth decay as a result of crunching sugary candy as a kid. I used to allow that sugar to remain lodged in my teeth all day long until eventually it caused my pearly whites to deteriorate and rot. Of course, drinking 200 ounces of Coke everyday for most of my adult years probably didn't help matters much either!

Another adverse effect sugar has on the body is it makes you hyperactive, especially in children. Sugar has long been a source of concern for parents with disruptive children who can't concentrate in school and seem to overflow with energy that has to come out of them somehow. A lot of kids who have been diagnosed with such conditions as attention deficit disorder and hyperactivity are likely victims of eating too much sugar in their diet. Rather than giving these kids prescription drugs that can harm them, how about cutting sugar out of the foods they eat to see how they react? I bet it would help solve the behavioral problems in many of them.

Think about it. If sugar can cause this much psychological and physical chaos in a child, then why do we choose to feed our kids any sugar at all?! Furthermore, why do we set a bad example for our children by eating a lot of sugar ourselves?

Most of us eat sugar because frankly we like the rush it gives us when we want to relax and enjoy something sweet to eat. It makes us happy and gives us a sense of euphoria whenever we taste the sweetness that comes from sugar. Eating sugar to make yourself feel better is counterproductive, though, because you actually end up feeling worse when you blood sugar rapidly increases and then suddenly drops. The end result is you start to feel jittery and on edge. This is not exactly my idea of a relaxing experience. Isn't it ironic that what we actually experience when we eat sugar is the exact opposite of what we had hoped would happen? Is the temporary thrill we get from sugar really worth the crash and burn that follows?

So, here's my question for you: Have you thought about giving up sugar completely yet? Do you realize how harmful it is to your body?

If you are now convinced that you need to abandon your sugar addiction for good, then I know you are wondering if you will ever be able to eat sweets again, right? My quick answer to that question is absolutely and I'll tell you how.

People often ask me, "What do you do about the need to eat something sweet? How can you live without any sugar at all?" That's a funny question when I hear it because I don't live without sweets. What I choose to live without is sugar. A lot of people think if you give up sugar then you also have to give up tasty treats such as candy bars, desserts and even chocolate. This is just not true. There are some days that I have eaten as much as a pound of chocolate while livin' la vida low-carb. I have enjoyed every luscious bite and did not feel guilty about it one bit!

However, I am simply not interested in eating or drinking anything sweetened with the overloaded amounts of sugar they put in foods today when there are so many delectable sugar-free desserts available. In my opinion, these taste just as good if not better than the ones with sugar in them. If people would just stop for a moment and taste how incredibly good these candies and desserts really are, then they would never go back to sugar again!

Have you tasted the low-carb candies from Russell Stover? Oh my goodness, all I can think about when I eat these is how much I'm "suffering" again on my diet! These candies are so incredibly delicious and worth every penny for their great taste.

My boss at work is funny because she is one of those people who believes anything labeled "sugar-free" must taste gross. What's up with that? Why do people automatically assume that something devoid of sugar can't taste sweet? While sugar-free desserts may not have any sugar in them, they do contain excellent sugar substitutes. These artificial sweeteners are so much better tasting than the ones we grew up with (Do you remember the funky-looking liquid Ril-Sweet bottles at restaurants twenty years ago? My dad used that in his restaurants and that stuff was so gross!). They satisfy your need for the taste of sugar without giving you any of the adverse side effects I've previously outlined earlier in this chapter about consuming the real thing. The amazing technological advances in the sugar substitutes these days completely eradicates any need to ever use sugar again.

The following sugar substitutes are the five most popular ones on the market today and are listed in the order I would recommend that you try them:

TOP FIVE SUGAR SUBSTITUTES ON THE MARKET TODAY:

1. SUCRALOSE (sold as Splenda)

This is the first sugar substitute I would recommend you use when you are livin' la vida low-carb. The most popular artificial sweetener on the market today comes remarkably close to matching the flavor of sugar and can be used as a great substitution for sugar in any recipe. It does not have any calories and is found in literally thousands upon thousands of products in your grocery store. Look for the familiar Splenda symbol.

There has been a lot of scrutiny about Splenda over the past year regarding its safety for consumers. But in study after study of this product, it has been found to be a completely safe alternative to sugar. Interestingly, most of the organized attacks against Splenda have been funded by none other than the Sugar Association. Do you think they're starting to feel the sting of those of us who are livin' la vida low-carb?

2. STEVIA

This plant-based sugar substitute is not as prevalent in the marketplace as Splenda is, but it is another excellent artificial sweetener for people following a low-carb plan. It contains 300 times the sweetness of sugar. You may not be able to find this sugar substitute in your local grocery store because it isn't sold as a name-brand product like the other sugar substitutes are. Look for it in the supplement section at virtually any natural or health food store.

3. ACESULFAME POTASSIUM (aka Ace-K, sold as Sunnet and Sweet One)

This sugar substitute provides the sweetness in products such as Diet Rite, Diet Coke with Splenda, and Coke Zero to give them a rich and flavorful sugar-like taste like nothing you've ever tried. This sweetener is 200 times sweeter than sugar and is also good for using in your favorite dessert recipes. It is usually combined with Splenda to add a distinctively sweet flavor to diet beverages.

4. SACCHARIN (sold as Sweet 'n Low)

Affectionately called "the pink stuff" and long thought to cause cancer in people, this sugar substitute has made a comeback of sorts since the Food & Drug Administration declared it safe for people to use a few years ago. It's still got a funny aftertaste to me, but provides 300 times the sweetness of sugar. However, it is not recommended to be used as a substitute in cooking recipes requiring sugar because it doesn't work well when heated.

5. ASPARTAME (aka Nutrasweet and sold as Equal)

This used to be the artificial sweetener used most often by companies that sold sugar-free and low-sugar products before Splenda overtook that title from them in 2005. While it provides about 180 times the sweetness of sugar, I do not recommend this artificial sweetener. Since there are so many other sugar substitutes to satisfy your need for sweetness, I believe you should try to avoid products made with aspartame when you are on a low-carb lifestyle if at all possible. Also, it cannot be used in any cooking recipes because it breaks down at higher temperatures.

Keep in mind that some people have difficulty with certain artificial sweeteners which can cause them to experience some adverse side effects, such as massive headaches and body aches. If you experience any physiological changes from consuming sugar substitutes, then try another one instead. The last thing you need to do is let one bad artificial sweetener cause you to go back to sugar again. That would be a big mistake.

In addition to these artificial sweeteners, there are also sugar alcohols frequently used to make the sugar-free products you buy taste so good. Some examples of the most popular sugar alcohols, which subsequently can be subtracted from your total carbohydrates when you are following a low-carb eating plan

(WOO-HOO!) include sorbitol, xylitol, erythritol, maltitol and lactitol.

While I did not personally have any problems with my weight stalling by consuming a lot of products with sugar alcohols in them, some people are not so lucky. I would caution you about eating too much of anything with sugar alcohols or artificial sweeteners because they may increase your cravings for sugar. Again, this was not my experience, but I thought you should be aware of how your body could react to these.

You also have to be careful about eating too many sugar-free foods made with the ingredients maltitol and lactitol because they can cause you to experience excessive gas (and that's not a comfortable feeling as I quickly found out when I first started eating low-carb candies). It's a little demented to think about, but this side effect can also work as a built-in control mechanism to keep you from overindulging on these sugar-free delights if you know your tummy will hurt after eating too many of them.

Another thing to watch out for is assuming that a product with the Splenda symbol on the front of the package makes it safe to consume. You have to read the ingredients in the product carefully to see if it uses sugar alcohols more prominently instead. Be aware of this deceptive marketing tactic companies use to get you to buy their products. If you notice the ingredient sucralose is at or near the bottom of the ingredients list while maltitol or lactitol are near the top, then it's probably not a very good product to buy. If you see maltitol syrup as the very first ingredient on a sugar-free product, then you might want to put it back in favor of one that does not cause the stomach issues.

If you want to avoid this feeling altogether, then you can either limit the amount of sugar-free candies you eat with maltitol or lactitol in them or look for products that are made with erythritol, such as Z-Carb chocolate bars (www.zcarb.com), which do not cause any gastric distress when they are consumed. My favorite flavor is dark chocolate and these are very delicious if you like chocolate. Check 'em out!

Sugar-free product manufacturers are going to have to come to terms with their overuse of sugar alcohols such as maltitol and lactitol. While I personally enjoy the taste of Russell Stover's low-carb candies and they have grown their line of products into top sellers, they will need to come up with another way to sweeten their sugar-free products if they expect sales to continue to be strong. I know a lot of people who cannot tolerate the adverse effects of those sugar alcohols and cannot buy these candies for that reason. They need to start sweetening their products with erythritol and Splenda instead and make us low-carbers happy campers.

There is something that I believe is even worse than sugar alcohols because it is an even greater nemesis to your goal of losing and maintaining weight loss. Unfortunately, this detriment to your low-carb lifestyle has already begun to pop up in a lot of foods alleging to be "low-carb." I'm referring to hidden sugars.

Food companies are very sneaky because they try to fool unsuspecting consumers who are following a low-carb approach by describing their products as "low-carb" or "low-sugar," but then putting more sugar in them than you really need. Even if you don't recognize these hidden sugars in the list of ingredients on the label, be sure you carefully read the nutritional label to find out how much sugar is in the product. Also pay close attention to the serving size since that will determine how much sugar you are actually putting in your body.

For example, the Carb-Alternative Kit-Kat bars have 10 grams of sugar in them per serving. While that is certainly lower than what a regular Kit-Kat contains, it's still too much when you are watching your carb intake, especially during the weight loss phase. Don't let these hidden sugars, which are nothing more than extra carbs you don't need, derail you from the success you deserve when you are on the low-carb lifestyle.

The best way to avoid the snare of hidden sugars is to just not buy anything that has more than just a little bit of sugar in it. Duh! That's not too difficult to follow, is it? Read the label and if it has more than a gram or two of sugar in it, then you need to put it back on the shelf. It's not worth blowing you whole low-carb program on useless carbs like that! Sugar is rat poison, remember?!

Some people have told me they worry about me eating so too much low-carb candy because if I eat too much of it I'll gain back my weight. Say what? How absurd can you get! Why do some people assume that people like me living a low-carb lifestyle will automatically start eating a lot more candy just because the amount of carbs in it is lower than ones containing sugar? While I guess I can understand the temptation some may have to binge on these tasty treats (they are legal after all and very low in carbs), I have learned to moderate my intake of these items and have found that I don't really need as much of them as I once did during my weight loss phase. Your body will adjust as you change your eating habits during your low-carb plan.

Even still, I have enjoyed eating low-carb candies since starting my low-carb lifestyle and have considered them a lifesaver for me during times when I really needed something sweet and to satisfy my desire for chocolate! People ask me if I miss chocolate and I tell them I can still eat all the chocolate I want. The difference now is I eat ones without any sugar in them.

I have to admit that I am very disappointed in the restaurant industry for failing to step up to the plate to offer people who are livin' la vida low-carb as well as diabetics the sugar-free desserts we want and need. While many restaurants either have a low-carb menu or are accommodating to making substitutions on the main course, they have been noticeably silent when it comes to an end of the meal treat.

There is one notable exception to this: Ruby Tuesday. This company has the most delicious sugar-free cheesecake you have every eaten in your entire life. In fact, it was so good that they got rid of their regular sugar-sweetened cheesecake in favor of this one made with a proprietary blend of artificial sweeteners and also has a delectable lightly cinnamon-flavored, nut-based crust. The best part is it only contains 1g net carb and tastes great topped with fresh strawberries or blueberries and whipped topping. I've even melted Z-Carb bars on top of this cheesecake. The only drawback is the price. It costs $5 for a slice, but you can buy an entire cheesecake with 12 slices for only $30. It's worth every single penny of it, too! Thank you, Ruby Tuesday, for getting it and providing us low-carbers with a dessert we can love and enjoy!

Some have scoffed at these low-carb desserts by claiming they have no redeeming value or benefit to people who are trying to lose weight. I'll tell you what is no benefit to people is all the sugar-laced, carb-loaaded foods they stuff their faces with on a daily basis. Where is the outcry about that? If as much energy was expended on the detrimental role sugar has played in the obesity epidemic in the United States, then maybe a solution would finally emerge that could restore the health of the citizens of our country.

Of course, a real solution already exists. It's called livin' la vida low-carb!

A survey released by the Grocery Manufacturers Association in May 2005 found that nearly half of grocery shoppers are looking for products made with less sugar. This gives me hope that the tide is finally turning and people are realizing the dangers of eating too much sugar.

Keep in mind that if something has very little or no sugar in it at all, then it is usually an excellent choice for people who are on a low-carb lifestyle. But don't rely on the front of food labels alone to give you all the information you need about making the right choices about whether or not a product is low in sugar. You have to turn the products over and read the nutritional content to find out the truth about the sugar found in that particular food item.

There's something else you need to know about food companies: they don't care about your health. All they care about is their bottom line and how to turn an even greater profit by creating the perception that they have products for people on a low-carb lifestyle. Some of them do make superb low-carb products, but most companies only pretend that they do. Read the nutritional information carefully before buying anything for your low-carb program.

Currently, there isn't a standardized policy in place that regulates what products can be described as "low-carb" or "low-sugar" on the grocery shelves. While I do not advocate the government getting involved in this process, I would like to see an independent organization or board of genuine low-carb experts create a universal criteria to be implemented regarding products that claim to be "low-carb" or "low-sugar."

Representatives from various low-carb companies and leaders in the low-carb community should be the ones to judge whether a product can be allowed to be called "low-carb" or "low-sugar" by establishing clear carbohydrate and sugar guidelines that must be followed by food manufacturers before something could be given that illustrious label. I personally think any product that has more than 2 grams of sugar per serving in it has no business at all being described as "low-carb."

If we're going to be serious about truth in advertising regarding "low-carb" and "low-sugar" products, then this is something that must be taken into immediate consideration. It would certainly cut down on the glut of low-carb products that have failed so miserably because they have not helped people trying to do a low-carb lifestyle. Who is going to lead the charge to make this simple idea into a reality?

What is incredibly ironic about this topic of sugar is how remarkably silent the low-fat supporters are about it. Isn't it a bit odd that you don't hear anyone criticizing the low-fat diets for actually promoting foods with enormous amounts of sugar in them? Get this! A regular Coca-Cola has zero grams of fat, but gobs and gobs of sticky, unhealthy sugar in it. Someone on a low-fat diet might surmise from reading the nutritional label that they can drink all the Cokes in the world they want since they don't contain any fat. What a big mistake in judgment that would be!

Of course, now we have medical researchers claiming that diet soda is actually worse for you to drink than regular soda. The University of Texas Health Science Center released a study in June 2005 that claims there is a 41 percent increased risk of becoming overweight or obese for each can or bottle of diet soda drank each day.

I guess my risk of being overweight or obese instantly increases by over 500 percent every single day because I drink 10-12 diet soft drinks in a typical day! All I can say is how incredibly thankful I was to have diet soda to drink as I was in the midst of losing my 180 pounds on the low-carb lifestyle. They were a real godsend to this former Cokeaholic! Although I still drink a lot of diet sodas, I also drink a lot of water, too. Most importantly, my weight has not been adversely affected one bit by my heavy consumption of diet sodas.

Yet another dirty little secret about low-fat diets is that most of the products they create are loaded with added sugars and sodium in an attempt to as closely as possible replicate the taste of the original versions of various foods. The resulting product is usually something that tastes very disgusting and introduces even more unnecessary sugar into your diet that you could live without. If you're trying to cut sugar out of your daily food intake, then you can't be doing that on a low-fat diet!

That's yet another reason why you should be on the low-carb lifestyle like the millions and millions of us who have already had great success with it. You can cut your sugar while enjoying lots of tasty foods that you simply can't have on a low-fat diet! It's the best thing I've ever done in my entire life because I was able to shrink my waistline and improve my overall health by ridding my body of sugar for good.

The bottom line is this: Sugar is not good for you at all. You need to do whatever you can to avoid it completely, especially when you are on a low-carb lifestyle. Even just a little bit of sugar can kick you out of ketosis and foil your plans to lose and maintain your weight. If everyone in this country would just cut sugar out of their lives, I contend we would see the obesity numbers plummet to near single digits!

While the media has focused much of their attention on fat consumption, especially with their criticism of people on a low-carb lifestyle, I believe they need to turn their attention to sugar consumption, generally associated with people on a low-fat diet. The truth is that we can live without sugar. It might be difficult for many to break their addiction, but it is something that must be done to restore the health and well-being of those Americans suffering from being overweight and obese.

Besides, sugar is rat poison and don't you forget it either!

KEY POINTS TO REMEMBER FROM CHAPTER 6:

- You must immediately give up eating sugar
- When tempted by a sugary dessert, think of it as rat poison
- Don't underestimate the effect sugar has had on your weight problem
- Break your sugar addiction to avoid harmful side effects
- Use sugar substitutes to make foods taste sweet
- Be careful about eating too much low-carb candy with sugar alcohols
- Beware of hidden sugars, even in so-called "low-carb" foods
- Use low-carb/sugar-free candy in moderation to satisfy your sweet tooth
- Don't buy any product with more than 2 grams of sugar per serving
- Realize that low-fat products have a lot more sugar in them than low-carb products

Chapter 7
Creativity Keeps It Interesting

If I've heard it once, then I've heard it a million times from so many different people attempting to describe what they think about the low-carb lifestyle (as if anybody really cares!).

It generally goes a little something like this:

"Eating low-carb is just so boring! Don't you get tired of eating just meat, cheese and eggs all the time? How can you purposely make something so monotonous and mundane an interesting way to eat?"

Oh, brother! Where do you even try to begin with such nonsense? If one more person criticizes the low-carb way of eating as a drab, unexciting, and utterly boring plan for weight loss and weight maintenance, then I think I'm gonna scream (okay, maybe I won't scream out loud, but I'll think about it really hard!). Or, as former presidential candidate and Democratic National Committee Chairman Howard Dean might say, "YAAAHHHHHHH!"

Well, I guess if all I ever ate was meat, cheese and eggs, then undoubtedly I would quickly get tired of my low-carb plan just as anybody would. How incredibly robotic would your life be if you were forced to eat nothing but the same old foods day after day after day?

Thankfully, there's a whole lot more excitement in your dining options when you are livin' la vida low-carb than being forced to just eat meat, cheese and eggs all day. Seriously! All you have to do is put on your creative cap every once in a while and add a little bit of your own personality and tastes into what you decide to put in your mouth to spice it up just a bit.

Getting creative with your low-carb lifestyle is an absolutely essential element to attaining long-term success both during the weight loss phase and on into your weight maintenance. It is especially important to learn how to be creative in the early part of your low-carb program so when you eventually reach your weight loss goal in the near future (and you will make it!), then you will have already learned the skillful art of switching things up and trying something new every once in a while. If you do anything the exact same way for any length of time, then it is inevitable you will get bored with it. Don't let that happen to your low-carb program!

Are you one of those people who considers yourself creatively inept? Do you feel that you are clueless when it comes to coming up with new ideas to pump new life into your low-carb lifestyle when it starts to feel too routine? Then you will want to keep reading this chapter to find out exactly what you can do to continue making livin' la vida low-carb the exciting and incredibly interesting way of eating you expected it to be when you first started.

When it comes to describing the various diet plans out there today, there's only one program in my opinion that takes the prize as the number one most boring weight loss program on the planet. When you are on this particular diet, you are constantly hungry and you never get to eat anything that actually tastes good. You feel like you are depriving yourself of so many of your favorite foods on this plan (and you really are!). If you one of the few who are fortunate enough to actually lose weight on this diet, then you will likely be unable to sustain it for very long. What is this unbelievably ineffective diet called?

As I'm sure you've figured it out already -- it's the low-fat/low-calorie/portion-controlled diet!

While the media and medical professionals continually champion the supposed virtues of the low-fat diet approach, new research studies have shown it is not nearly as effective as the low-carb lifestyle. Additionally, participants in both of these diets report the quality and quantity of the foods eaten on a low-fat weight loss diet plan are not nearly as appealing or satisfying as those you can enjoy when you are on a low-carb program. In my experience on both a low-fat and a low-carb weight loss approach, watching your fat and calorie intake is a hundred times harder to keep up with and a lot less desirable to implement into your life than watching your carbohydrates!

Hmmm, should I choose the low-fat diet and eat a salad or pick low-carb and savor a tender, juicy steak instead? Which would you prefer if you had your choice? There's just no comparison.

Are you looking for real variety in your weight loss program? Then eating low-carb is definitely the way to go! The selection of foods on a low-carb lifestyle not only taste so much better than those on low-fat, but are also more plentiful in the grocery store than low-fat foods are. I think any logical-thinking person would want to have greater variety in their eating choices, not less. Furthermore, you don't have to worry about putting anything in your mouth like fat-free luncheon meats ever again if you choose low-carb living (I have nightmares just thinking about it!).

My own personal experience on so many different diet plans over the years has given me ample opportunity to evaluate the good from the not-so-good. Although you can have weight loss success on virtually any diet program, I have discovered that eating a low-fat diet is a lot less desirable and much more difficult to maintain than eating the low-carb way. If a diet gets to be too boring and you can't keep it up, then all the weight you tried so hard to lose will come rushing back on you in a very short amount of time. That's exactly what happened to me when I was on a low-fat diet.

In 1999, when I lost 170 pounds on a low-fat diet, my food selection was limited mostly to fat-free (or should a say taste-free!) foods of all kinds that contained an inordinate amount of extra salt and sugar in them supposedly to make them taste as close to the original products as possible. Obviously that game plan didn't work! To this day I don't know how I ever convinced myself to eat those foods!

I often ended up eating a salad with a portion-controlled serving of fat-free Thousand Island or fat-free Ranch dressing as a typical meal on my low-fat diet. While I actually like a good salad when I'm in the mood for one, this same old rabbit food meal got old very quickly. What made it even worse was all the other fat-free foods that tasted absolutely disgusting and left me unsatisfied and hungry.

Just in case you are wondering, I do eat salads today. I admit that I didn't eat very many of them when I first started livin' la vida low-carb because they reminded me too much of being on a low-fat diet. But now, unlike the salads I had to eat then, I make sure I doctor them up with lots of cheese, boiled eggs, turkey, ham, bacon, and full-fat Ranch dressing on them. Yummy to my tummy!

That's the thing about low-fat diets. They make you get so ravenously hungry! And my wife can tell you that when I am hungry, I get irritable. I'm sure I drove her crazy that year I was on my low-fat diet. It was not a pleasant experience for me despite my weight loss success. There was literally nothing I could enjoy on my low-fat diet, so I got extremely bored with it and always desired to eat foods that I loved and enjoyed. That menacing negative thought process ultimately led to my miserable failure on the low-fat diet, even after losing 170 pounds.

A low-fat diet does not allow you to be creative because you are stuck eating many foods you really don't want or desire. This is not true with low-carb. In fact, just the opposite is true. You have so many foods you can experiment with that you'll constantly be coming up with new concoctions and recipes to make your low-carb lifestyle that much more interesting.

Additionally, while I may not have been consuming very much fat when I was on my low-fat diet, I was certainly loading up on a lot of extra carbs I didn't need and was not enjoying the foods I was being forced to eat. My body obviously craved the extra protein and fats that I now get from my low-carb lifestyle to take away my hunger and keep my weight off for good. You can be hard-headed like I was and try the failed low-fat diet or you can be wise and choose to follow the low-carb approach to attain permanent weight loss success at last.

As I stated previously, after about a year of eating a low-fat diet and being constantly hungry, I started eating "normal" again because I was tired of depriving myself of so many wonderful foods that I loved to eat and enjoy. My wife recalls the day I told her I wanted to order a Big Mac value meal from McDonald's and she instinctively knew at that moment that my low-fat diet was finished. She was right because it all went down hill from there!

The weight loss was nice, but eating a low-fat diet for the rest of my life was simply asking too much from me. I don't know anyone who eats this way all the time. I tried my best to be as creative as I possibly could with the food choices I had at my disposal, but a low-fat diet was just not a sustainable way to eat over the long-term.

Furthermore, I did not feel good about the way I was eating on a low-fat diet because I always felt like I was starving myself. Although I was a smaller man as a result of the weight loss, I knew the method I had used to lose weight was not healthy for me. There was no way I was going to eat that way until the day God took me home. Some days I felt so awful while I was on a low-fat diet that I sometimes wished I could die because life is not worth living in such misery.

Now fast forward to 2004. Throwing out all of the lies that I had ever heard about low-carb and forever leaving the world of "fat-free" behind, I started livin' la vida low-carb on New Year's Day because I was licking my lips at all the possibilities I could create using so many of the foods I loved. The bonus was that I could still eat those foods and lose weight, too. Yee haw! What more could I ask for (well, chocolate cake would have been nice, but I quickly learned to put it down for good for the sake of better health!)?

During those first two weeks on the Induction phase, it was only slightly boring inasmuch as the limitations on what you are allowed to eat during this essential stage of your low-carb lifestyle are at their strictest for this very short amount of time. But your body is required to go through some significant changes and adjustments to begin losing weight and sacrificing a mere fourteen days really isn't too much to ask. I didn't think it was.

Additionally, you mind and body have to adjust to this radically different way of eating you enjoy when on low-carb because it won't feel like a diet. For the first time ever, you are actually able to eat some foods that have traditionally been taboo on most "normal" (translated "low-fat") diets.

You will be able to enjoy eating foods such as butter, cream, hamburgers, steak and other high fat/high protein delights. There's certainly an adjustment period you need to go through psychologically in order to change the way you think about these types of foods (i.e. thinking they are bad for you, etc.) so you can eventually see a real change physiologically when you eventually find success on your low-carb lifestyle.

A major part of that transformation of the mind includes getting creative with the low-carb foods you can eat. You don't have to be a world-renowned chef to come up with all sorts of interesting food combinations, but you do have to have a passion to do everything possible to keep both the foods you eat and the way you eat as interesting as you can while you are livin' la vida low-carb.

Nobody (and I mean nobody!) is going to do this for you. You must be the one to decide for yourself if you want low-carb to be drab and boring or if you want it to be the most unbelievably exciting way to lose weight and keep it off that you've ever tried! The choice you make can and will ultimately decide whether or not you are successful on low-carb.

Despite the tidal wave of negative media reports about the alleged demise of the low-carb "fad" because of a lack of sales of foods labeled "low-carb," there are still so many foods on the supermarket shelves today that are naturally low-carb and don't need to be labeled that way to suddenly make them acceptable for someone on the low-carb lifestyle. With the way the low-carb lifestyle is being reported in the media these days, you would think nobody is doing it. But try telling that to the tens of millions of us who are happily livin' la vida low-carb today and will be for many years to come!

While the "low-carb" labels have been helpful to those people who are new to this way of eating because it makes it somewhat easier to identify food choices on a low-carb program, I still encourage people to read nutrition labels for themselves to look for those foods that are actually low in carbohydrates. This also forces you to be creative in the way you buy the foods you are eating on your low-carb lifestyle.

In fact, why don't you make it a game the next time you visit the grocery store? Here's what you should do: start walking up and down the aisles looking for any product that has the word "carb" on the front of the package. Pick it up, turn it over on the side or back where the nutrition information is located and look at the total carbs minus the dietary fiber and sugar alcohols. Taking into account the serving size, determine if that product is something that you would feel comfortable eating based on the net carbs. If it doesn't, then you need to put it back.

My rule of thumb is to always reject anything that had double-digit net carbs in it because the carbs in those products add up way too quickly. There are so many other low-carb foods you can purchase that won't waste the number of carbs you can eat in a day.

You can even try using this shopping method on foods that aren't labeled "low-carb" and will be astounded by the excessive amount of carbohydrates that are found in so many of the foods you can buy on supermarket shelves. Is it any wonder why two-thirds of Americans are overweight or obese?

Another creative way to keep your low-carb plan interesting is to buy one new product you haven't tried before once a week. You still want to make sure it stays within your allowable carbs parameter, but get something new you've never had before. This is so exciting, too!

You could decide to finally try that low-carb pasta you always wondered about. I remember how hesitant I was about purchasing Dreamfield's pasta for the first time because it actually looked like it would taste good compared with the horror stories I had heard from other low-carbers about how gross some of the "other" low-carb pasta brands were. But once I took the plunge and tasted Dreamfield's for myself, oh my goodness, I was hooked and now make it a regular part of my low-carb lifestyle!

You might want to try those low-carb brownies or even the low-carb chocolate chip cookies that have been staring at you every time you go to the grocery store. The Atkins brand of both of these products really surprised me by their high quality and great taste. You'll never know how good something might be until you decide to try it for yourself. Take a chance and constantly try new low-carb products! I guarantee it will keep your low-carb lifestyle interesting for a very long time.

Better yet, here is another challenge for you that will also spark your creativity on your low-carb lifestyle. Try shopping around in a variety of stores you don't normally visit. You will be amazed by the wide selection of low-carb foods that varies from store to store, even in the same town. All supermarkets don't necessarily carry the same products. Look around and I bet you will find something different from each store that will allow you to expand your low-carb menu far beyond what it is now.

For a while I was dismayed because I couldn't find the Atkins bread at my usual grocery store. But after visiting one of their local competitors, I saw an entire display full of exactly what I was looking for. While I was there I also happened to find a low-carb pita bread and some low-carb wraps that I had never tried before and now they have become regular items I buy for my low-carb lifestyle. I frequent this particular store often just to get these unique and delicious items I am looking for.

Whatever it is that tickles your fancy or floats you boat, just give it a try. Pretty soon you'll have so many favorite low-carb foods to choose from that you'll have a tough time deciding which ones to purchase. Hey, wait a minute! I thought they said low-carb was boring! Obviously it's not when you get creative!

The fact of the matter is we live in a fast-paced, thrill-me-now society that quickly gets bored with just about anything and wants something new all the time. We demand excitement in virtually every area of our lives, especially with the foods we decide to put in our mouths. If your food choices on your low-carb way of eating get boring, then you need to stir up your creative juices and make it interesting again. There are many other ways you can do that, too!

Try reading a low-carb recipe book or hop on the Internet and go surfing for new recipes that interest you (might I suggest you visit the Kalyn's Kitchen blog at kalynskitchen.blogspot.com). Low-carb ideas are plentiful, but you have to do a little research for yourself. It is your responsibility alone to constantly think of ways to keep the same vigor and passion for low-carb that you had when you first began. Otherwise, like I said before, you are destined to fail at attaining the weight loss you are striving so hard to achieve and then keeping it off as you deserve.

The media has grown very tired of the low-carb lifestyle and have apparently decided to make it their mission to completely destroy anything and everything positive that comes out about it. They are constantly talking about how it is just a "fad" that is finally coming to an end. Quoting marketing analysts, economists, nutritionists, doctors and whoever else they can find, the journalists who write these stories are trying to convince people to move on from the low-carb "craze" because there are supposedly much more exciting diets to try.

For example, they've fallen all over themselves over a book called The 3 Hour Diet by Jorge Cruise which suggests people should eat low-fat/low calorie foods every three hours to lose weight. How much more absurd can you get than a diet like this?! Even if I was allowed to eat those nasty-tasting low-fat foods 24 hours a day for seven days a week, it still wouldn't make me want to do it! Oh, but it's the latest and greatest thing, so it must be worth promoting! Oi!

You may have noticed a sudden transition from foods being labeled "low-carb" to the newest food marketing trend that started happening at the beginning of 2005. While food manufacturers once couldn't wait to plaster the phrase "low-carb" on all their products when it was at its height of popularity in 2004, now the key words seem to be "sugar-free" and "low-sugar." The media apparently got bored with the term "low-carb" and I predict they'll soon get just as tired with "low-sugar" as well. Just give them a little while. Their impatience will begin to show up in a negative article here and there until the negativity will begin to rapidly spread across the media like it has with low-carb.

Nevertheless, despite the media's attempts to destroy low-carb, this way of eating is not going anywhere anytime soon as people who are livin' la vida low-carb are still trucking along. We choose to ignore the media's attempts to taint and smear our eating lifestyle choice because we have grown to love low-carb for the weight loss success we have had on it.

While the media may have convinced many of the food companies to change their product packaging because of their reports of the demise of low-carb, they haven't changed the minds of us low-carbers because we know the way we are choosing to eat is the right plan of action for us. The sudden disappearance of foods labeled "low-carb" will only force us to continue to be creative in our shopping, but that will not stop us from doing this for the rest of our lives. It's a whole lot more interesting when you have to think about the kinds of foods you need for your low-carb lifestyle than to simply rely on information that may not be accurate on the packaging.

One of the primary reasons people think low-carb is boring stems from the mistaken notion that you hardly eat any carbs on the program. Contrary to popular belief, low-carb does not mean no-carb. You never go completely without any carbs while you are on a low-carb program (except for people who are on the Induction phase of the South Beach Diet). While you are restricted to about 20g of carbohydrates during the first couple of weeks on most low-carb plans, you certainly don't stay there. In the subsequent weeks, you begin purposely adding back a plethora of foods chock full of good carbohydrates that you can have and enjoy while livin' la vida low-carb. Yet, the media chooses to ignore this undeniable fact about low-carb and instead creates lies about how the program really works. These dishonest tactics are a disservice to people who are trying educate themselves about healthy living.

If cravings for certain kinds of foods are driving you crazy, then I encourage you to find low-carb versions to satisfy those urges. If you miss bread, then try the Atkins-approved low-carb bread. If ice cream is your weakness, then you'll be pleasantly surprised by the many excellent flavors from nearly every ice cream manufacturer out there. Choices abound when you are on a low-carb lifestyle.

Of course, just as you should experiment by purchasing at least one new low-carb product a week, likewise you should also try out a new low-carb recipe on a weekly basis. Many of these are readily available on the Internet and in books. Find one that looks good to you and give it a whirl. If it is a good recipe that you really liked, then add it to your list of regular food choices for yet another selection to choose from on your low-carb menu. That's what I did with my low-carb chocolate peanut butter cheesecake balls and my chicken bacon ranch melt (you can find these recipes at the end of Chapter 1), both of which I make on a regular basis.

Speaking of the Internet, fresh new ideas about the low-carb lifestyle are just about everywhere online. I have highlighted many different web sites on my blog that offer encouragement for people following low-carb, post reviews and opinions about the latest news and books about low-carb, as well as link you up with other people just like me who have been successful at implementing the low-carb lifestyle as a permanent weight loss and weight maintenance solution. Go to livinlavidalowcarb.blogspot.com to find even more creative ideas about low-carb that will keep this way of eating interesting for you.

If all of that is not enough to get your creative juices flowing, then you can always send me a comment or question and I'll do my best to help you keep your low-carb lifestyle interesting. You can e-mail me at livinlowcarbman@charter.net.

It's time for you to get energized and excited about creativity so you'll never fool yourself into believing that "eating low-carb is just so boring!" Now you know better.

KEY POINTS TO REMEMBER FROM CHAPTER 7:

- Realize that low-carb is so much more than eating meat, cheese and eggs
- Don't eat or do the same things all the time on your low-carb lifestyle
- Think about how incredibly boring and tasteless low-fat diets are
- Decide for yourself that you will make low-carb interesting
- Make shopping for low-carb foods a game by reading the nutrition labels
- Pick out a new low-carb food to try every week
- Ignore the media's attempt to convince you low-carb is boring
- If you miss a certain kind of food, find a low-carb version to eat

- Try a new low-carb recipe once a week
- Look for creative ideas about low-carb on the Internet

Chapter 8
A Support System That Sustains You

The topic of this chapter will attempt to explain why so many people who have tried to lose weight have inevitably failed to reach their goals. Many people just completely underestimated the significance of a support system in both achieving and sustaining their weight loss.

I have no doubt in my mind that you must make a conscious effort to surround yourself with people who will reinforce your new eating choices as well as encourage you to continue on with your weight loss plan, especially when you don't feel like doing it anymore. Believe me, those days will come.

Nevertheless, the importance of having people in your life who will serve as your support system cannot be overstated because they will literally sustain you throughout your entire weight loss experience. Whether it is the good, the bad or the ugly, these are the people who will never stop believing in you to reach your weight loss goals. They will stand by your side every step of the way.

I can think of so many people who helped me in my own weight loss journey and I want to mention just a few of them by name in this chapter because they share just as much in my victory over my weight problem as I do. Without them, I don't think my weight loss would have been possible. These are very special people who mean all the world to me. I will never forget how they cheered me on to victory over my weight problem.

First and foremost, let me say that my faith in God was what truly sustained me the most above everything else during my weight loss. There would be times when I would pray to the Lord and humbly ask Him to provide me with an extra dose of strength to get me through the day in those moments when the challenge to keep going forward was incredibly overbearing. I believe that allowing God Himself to be a part of my weight loss experience was an essential ingredient to my success.

I give my Lord and Saviour Jesus Christ all the glory and honor for allowing me to live and breathe each day and I acknowledge His grace and mercy on me before, during, and after my weight loss experience. It is my prayer that His name will be exalted in everything I do, including through my weight loss story and this book. He is worthy to be praised because of what He has done through my life and I admit that I am nothing without Him.

Throughout my weight loss journey, God so graciously allowed me to come into contact with various people who also played crucial roles in my success. They, in essence, became a part of my support system whether they realized it or not! There was one person in particular who was at the forefront of that group of people who provided me with exactly the kind of support that I needed to be able to do this. She was there when I lost 170 pounds on a low-fat diet in 1999 and was willing to go through all that again this time around on my low-carb program. Of course, I'm referring to my beautiful and loving wife, Christine.

Before I started my low-carb lifestyle, I asked Christine to be my accountability partner in this new endeavor. She gleefully accepted this role as she had been praying for me to do something about my weight problem for the entire time we have been married (2005 marked ten years of marital bliss!). There's no doubt in my mind that Christine was extremely skeptical of how well I would do when I first started livin' la vida low-carb because of my poor track record for keeping weight off that I have lost in the past. I've lost and regained so much weight in my lifetime that I stopped keeping track of it. I've probably lost and gain well over 1,000 pounds in my life. It's been a real rollercoaster ride!

Christine's gentle words of genuine encouragement were in sharp contrast to what I perceived as her "nagging" regarding my weight in the past. While what she was saying was veiled in language that made it sound like she was concerned about my health, all I could hear was YACK YACK YACK YACK YACK because I was fat! Anybody else know what I'm talking about here?

Let me pause for just a moment to focus on this issue because it is something that needs to be emphasized clearly to anyone who needs to lose weight.

I'm sure we've all had spouses, parents, children, and friends say something to us about our weight problem before, right? Why is it that we often feel like they are lashing out at us in vile hatred or with a judgmental attitude when they talk to us about our weight problem? Could it be that they actually do love us and want what is best for our health?

I know it is difficult to acknowledge that truth when you are the one who has the weight problem. But the reality of the situation is that you do have a weight problem that needs to be addressed. While I don't doubt there have been some people who may not have been as tactful as they need to be in their approach to you about your weight, the truth in their message should not be misconstrued or misunderstood. I know it can be hard to hear, but it is something that needs to be said.

In my life, there was a rather rotund, older lady named Elizabeth who didn't mind telling me at every opportunity about how big she thought I was. She often told me that I was fat and needed to lose weight. I used to get so angry at her insinuation that I had a weight problem when she was packing on quite a few extra pounds herself. How incredibly hypocritical, I used to think!

While that's a natural response that most people would have to being lectured about their weight from another overweight person, I eventually began to realize that people like her were actually serving as my cheerleaders in this neverending battle against the bulge. They really were rooting me on to reach the eventual success I would attain. You would be served well to have this attitude for yourself about those who would criticize you for being overweight, even if their words can be a bit abrasive at times.

Getting back to the role my wife Christine played in my weight loss, I can vividly remember when she used to come up to me with tears rolling down her cheeks and begging me to do something about my weight. But I wouldn't listen to her because I didn't want to hear about my weight problem. I already knew I was fat and didn't need someone to constantly remind me of that! I thought I was happy the way I was living and didn't need my wife to tell me otherwise.

But those were deep-seeded lies that I kept telling myself to put off losing weight and getting healthy. Why did I have to be so hard-headed about this? Didn't I realize my own wife was simply concerned that I might be on the road to an early grave?

It took me a few years to figure it out, but if finally clicked in my mind that this was something I needed to do for real this time. Otherwise, there may not be a next time.

When I finally reached the place in my life where I wanted to seriously get my weight problem under control, I knew I could count on Christine to step forward and hold me accountable. She was so excited that her husband was finally going to do something about his weight that she completely invested herself into this role. She did it with all the loving care and concern you would expect from a spouse. Be sure to read what Christine wrote about what it was like "Livin' With The Low-Carb Man" at the end of the book.

Looking back now, I could not have chosen a better accountability partner! Christine was absolutely fantastic because she knew exactly when I needed a gentle nudge forward and when to give me a big kick in the rear end to get me going! I will forever be thankful to her for helping me get through this incredible weight loss experience to become the new man that I am today. Christine, I'll love you forever and ever, bunny wunny pooky wooky bear say i-yi-yi, i-yi-yi (that's an inside joke between us -- don't ask)!

Do you have someone like Christine who can play this role in your weight loss pathway? It is absolutely essential that you team up with someone you trust who will be very honest with you and tell you what a great job you are doing or gently get on your case if you fall off the wagon. If someone is unwilling to do that, then you need to find someone who can.

Unlike other weight loss plans, when you are livin' la vida low carb you have something else you have to contend with that can keep you from staying committed to it. There will be plenty of people who will try to discourage you from engaging in the low-carb lifestyle because of the reasons I outlined in Chapter 5. That is why you need so many positive influences that will encourage, not discourage you. Surrounding yourself with people like this will make it much more likely that you will reach your weight loss goals and become the thin and healthy person you've always wanted to be.

Yet, I understand how very difficult it can be for some people who may not have very many close friends or family members to find the support system they need. Even still, this step is so essential in your weight loss journey that you should at least try to find a select group of people who can and will hold you accountable and allow them to lift you up when you are down as well as lovingly chastise you when you need to be put back on track.

Something rather peculiar happened to me as I began losing weight on my low-carb plan. The people I encountered on a daily basis suddenly began noticing my weight loss and started talking to me about it seemingly out of the blue. This even includes a whole lot of people who have never spoken a word to me ever before! Oh sure, I've seen their faces at work, church and in the community, but I had never actually officially met most of these people before my weight loss.

Strangely, these people began offering unsolicited praise and compliments about my weight loss because they finally noticed I was doing something about it. This is a very exciting part of the weight loss stage of livin' la vida low-carb and you should thoroughly enjoy it. Let their sweet words of support light a fire within you to keep doing it no matter what!

Interestingly, it wasn't until I had lost nearly 100 pounds before anybody even noticed I was losing weight! What took them so long to notice?! Hee hee! But don't let that discourage you from doing this for yourself. You can't get to the compliments stage of your weight loss experience until you've first put forth the effort that makes people realize you are serious this time around.

Whether you know it or not, people are watching you. They want you to succeed in your weight loss and are quietly rooting for you to stay strong and endure. But if you are like me, then you've lost weight before and gained it all back. It's gonna take a whole lot of convincing to friends and family that you really mean it this time and will keep the weight off for good. My friend Maude from church often asks me if I'm going to keep my weight off this time since she has seen me lose weight and gain it all back before. That's a fair question for her to ask. I assure her that I think I will because I'm livin' la vida low-carb now! She's one of many who are helping to keep me accountable and I'm thankful for that.

Be sure to remind yourself of that often, especially when you are first starting out on your low-carb lifestyle. Look at other people and imagine them saying encouraging phrases like, "You can do it!" Before long, you won't have to imagine it because they'll be verbalizing it to you. You'll see it firsthand if you can get the ball rolling forward on your weight loss.

It may have taken a little while, but the comments I started receiving from people during my weight loss were invaluable to my psyche as I continued losing weight. I needed to know that people thought I looked good and that I was doing well in my weight loss. I knew I had lost a lot of weight, but I wanted to hear it come from the lips of others. And, boy oh boy, did it ever (and it still does to this day!).

At first it seemed very strange to me when people would start calling me "skinny" and "thin man" at a time when I still felt in my mind that I was very fat. When you have been overweight for your entire life, it's hard to shake this negative sefl-image. But I allowed these positive comments to seep into my mind and slowly convince me that they are true because they are! That's the power of a strong support system. It's providing you with just the right word at just the right time to keep you going to reach the finish line in this race to better health.

In addition to my wife Christine, there were so many other people who touched my life in ways they will never know through a reassuring smile, a timely word, or just being there when I needed someone to talk to. These members of your support system can either make or break you in your weight loss endeavor. I am so fortunate that I was surrounded by a solid support system that helped me reach my weight loss goals and keep the weight off forever.

Here is just a brief listing of some of the people who helped me along the way in my 180-pound weight loss success story that I would like to recognize:

Rodney, a personal trainer at the YMCA I go to in Duncan, South Carolina, was always there with a big smile on his face asking me how my weight loss was going. The encouragement he gave me just by cheering me on to reach my goals was invaluable as I sought to lose weight and get into shape. Once I reached my weight loss goals, Rodney was also instrumental in starting me on a weight lifting schedule that has helped me grow muscles where I didn't know I had muscles and to tone up and tighten up areas of my body that needed it.

He once told me that while I often tell him how he has been an inspiration to me, he said that his observations of the hard work I invested into my weight loss and weight lifting training has been an enormous encouragement to him because it convicted him of his tendency to slack off on his own training. WOW! While most people would look at this man's very large muscles and think he's healthy and fit, he knew he needed to get back to the gym more often. I am glad to have been able to return the favor for this man I now call my friend. We hold each other accountable when we see each other in the gym now. Rodney, you da man! God bless you, my brother!

Gerry, my high-energy Sunday School teacher at church, started openly bragging about my weight loss in my Sunday School class and in front of other church members long before anybody else even noticed I was losing weight. He always asked about my "number," referring to the amount of weight I had lost.

After I reached 170 pounds lost, he told me that I had lost him, referring to his body weight. So that day I decided to give him a big bear hug and pick him up off the ground yelling, "This is what I used to weigh!" Gerry was always there with positive comments for me and kept me going throughout my weight loss experience. Thanks so much, Gerry! Your belief that I could do this was a real godsend that I'll not soon forget. I love you, man!

Harlan, an incredibly optimistic man of God, was another member of my church who noticed my weight loss before most others. He started calling me "Skinny" every time he would see me and said he would have to sometimes do a double-take because he wouldn't recognize me as I was losing weight. I started getting a lot of that especially after passing the 100-pound loss level.

But it was Harlan who started heaping praise on my efforts early and often. This special man with an incredible gift for uplifting others truly blessed me and motivated me with his infectious love and enthusiasm for my weight loss efforts. Harlan and his wife Sandy moved to Atlanta in early 2005, but I will never forget the long-term impact he made on my life. God bless you, Harlan, for being the Christlike example that you are and for loving me for who I was no matter how overweight I got.

Ann, who lost over 100 pounds on a nationally-known weight loss program, understood the struggles I was facing as an obese person. She used to have to walk with a cane and suffered from various joint and other health problems that inhibited her walking and overall physical well-being.

At about the same time I began my low-carb program, Ann went on a journey that helped her shed triple digits from her body and restore her health, too. We were always asking each other how our respective plans were working and encouraged each other to keep it up. Even today, Ann and I talk often and help hold each other accountable so we can both make sure our weight losses really are permanent. Ann, you hang in there girl because I know you can do it! You and I are living examples that weight loss can and will happen by the grace and mercy of God.

The girls at the office where I work, including Mary, Nicole, Bridget, Kathy, Cindy, Irene, Linda, Angela, Pat, and Angie, were always so gracious to me during my weight loss by making timely comments that would literally fuel me to the amazing success I had livin' la vida low-carb. It's a running joke that everybody in the department is dieting at some point or another. This is the same group of ladies who wonder why they don't lose any weight after scarfing down a box or two of doughnuts between them. Gee, I can't imagine why! Ha!

When they started noticing my weight loss, many of them began their own low-carb programs because I proved to them that the plan really works. Now this former 410-pounder is often asked for his advice about what to eat and other weight loss hints. I love these ladies because they have provided me with the daily dose of laughter and encouragement to get me through to the end of my weight loss and beyond. My prayer is that I can continue to be an example and motivation for them to reach their own personal weight loss goals. Never give up, ladies, never give up! I proved it can really happen! Now, get back to work!

Brenda, who is a devoted low-carber, was constantly providing me with new recipes, new low-carb foods, clothes her son couldn't fit into anymore, helpful advice for my low-carb lifestyle, and more. She had been on a low-carb lifestyle for several years before I started my own program, so it was nice to have a veteran show me the ropes about it.

After a while, I was able to return the favor and give her some tips that I had learned along my own low-carb path and now we often exchange information about new stores to shop at for low-carb foods and anything else that will help us continue the success we have had. Brenda, you were a true friend to me through this and I am thankful to have crossed paths with you.

D.R., my fellow contestant in the radio weight loss contest I was in, spurred me on in my own weight loss endeavor as I heard him talk about his success following the low-carb lifestyle, too. While we were competing against each other to win the prizes in "Ralph's Incredible Shrinking Ton" contest, I was silently cheering him on to do well, too.

Starting out at 619 pounds, he had a lot more weight to lose than I did. Just hearing him talk about his early success on the low-carb plan propelled me to new heights in my own weight loss. D.R., I pray you'll commit to continue this amazing journey of livin' la vida low-carb so you'll never ever have to suffer with the inevitable health problems associated with obesity. I believe in you, buddy! You can do it!

Ralph, the radio talk show host who conducted the weight loss contest, was gracious enough to allow me to be a part of the weight loss contest that I eventually won. When I would talk on the radio about my weight loss, Ralph was always extremely supportive and reassuring that I was doing something that would add years back to my life. He was right (but don't let that go to your head, Ralph!). I appreciate the continued support I have received from Ralph even since the weight loss contest concluded in November 2004.

When Ralph is out in the community at radio-sponsored events, he is always bragging about how much weight I have lost to people. Although he is the self-proclaimed "lonely voice of reason in a cacophony of chaotic chatter" in the Greenville/Spartanburg, SC market (shameless plug, shameless plug: tune in to WORD-AM 1330/950 and visit his web site at www.ralphbristol.com), Ralph still finds time to continue to check up on me to make sure I'm keeping my weight off. Thanks Ralph for all you've done to help me lose weight and keep it off! A special thank you for that extremely kind foreword to this book you wrote as well.

Nancy and Ben, managers at my favorite local dining spot, were eager to assist me with appropriate substitutions to a variety of menu items so I could make them low-carb. But even beyond that, they showed a genuine interest in my weight loss and that they cared about what I was doing.

It is very rare to find such people who work in the service industry that display these kind of unique character traits that Nancy and Ben showed me. I consider them friends and appreciate their assistance during my low-carb lifestyle. From the bottom of my heart, Nancy and Ben, I cannot thank you enough for the role you played in my weight loss success.

Finally, I want to recognize my Mom, who has struggled with her own weight problem throughout her entire life and decided to have gastric bypass surgery in December 2003. It was a difficult decision that she made for herself because she had reached the point where she did not see any other option that could work for her. Despite some complications after her surgery, she has lost well over 100 pounds and look fabulous!

Whether she knows it or not, my mother has always been my biggest supporter in whatever I have done. I'm so happy that she and I have found the weight loss we have been looking for. I'm so proud of you Mom and hope you will live a long and healthy life. Here's hoping that Kevin and Beverly (my brother and sister) can join us in our weight loss success in the coming years.

I'm sure there are many others I am leaving off of this abbreviated list of people who helped support me during my weight loss. There are so many people who will never even realize how the words they spoke to me at just the right time might have made all of the difference between me falling flat on my face or eventually attaining the weight loss success that I was able to reach.

From the bottom of my heart, I want to personally thank everyone who encouraged me during my weight loss. I celebrate your presence in my life during this incredible journey and thank God for how He used you to bring me to where I am today.

I anxiously await the opportunity to meet lots of new friends through this book and in other venues that I am allowed to explore as a result of my weight loss. We can all begin supporting others who need someone in their lives to show them it can be done. Working together, we can overcome this country's obesity problem once and for all.

What a ride it has been thanks to the support system that sustained me to lose 180 pounds and keep it off for good!

KEY POINTS TO REMEMBER FROM CHAPTER 8:

- Surround yourself with people who will reinforce your low-carb eating habits
- Find an accountability partner as soon as possible
- Allow God to strengthen you to endure in your weight loss
- When people criticize your weight, thank them for loving you enough to say something
- Stop lying to yourself about your weight and health problems and start doing something about it
- Heed the advice of your accountability partner even if it hurts
- Hang around people who will encourage, not discourage you in your low-carb lifestyle
- Enjoy the praise of those who will start noticing your weight loss and let it motivate you
- Acknowledge those people in your life who have inspired and encouraged you in your weight loss

- Be the support person for someone else who is struggling with a weight problem

Chapter 9
Perseverance To Reach Your Goals

In the midst of writing the previous chapter, something dramatic happened that perfectly illustrates the importance of the subject of this chapter on perseverance.

I was rolling along writing Chapter 8 and was almost finished with it when I attempted one Friday afternoon in June 2005 to open the word processor program I was using to write this book. I double clicked on the icon for the book and got an error message that stated the document could not be found. My heart immediately sunk! I backed out and tried it again, but I got the same result. I then shut down the computer completely and restarted the computer to see if that would let me bring it up. Nope.

Uh-oh! What in the world happened to my book?! AAAAAACK! Months and months of preparation and writing can't just disappear in an instant, can they? But that is exactly what I was facing because the file I saved it under was not opening.

What to do, what to do...

Scary thoughts began to enter my head and I didn't like any of them. How am I supposed to continue writing the book when it has just disappeared on me? Where could it have gone? Am I really going to have to rewrite the entire book from scratch? EEEEEK!

Thankfully, I have a friend named Jonathan who is an expert at figuring out computer problems and when I told him about it he informed me that the file I had my book saved under had likely become corrupted. I asked if it could be "uncorrupted" and he said he may be able to save it in part, but the information would very likely be garbled. I didn't really care what it looked like as long as I could salvage something from what I had written.

Yet when Jonathan went to retrieve it using his professional expertise, he was able to pull the entire document out unscathed except for a funky-looking font. What that meant was that I would have to retype the entire book, but that was a small price to pay to get the whole book back. My lovely wife Christine was gracious enough to retype the entire manuscript all over again so I could continue on with my writing. Isn't she so sweet?!

You may be asking yourself what this odd story about nearly losing my book has to do with perseverance in your low-carb lifestyle? Plenty.

There will be times during your weight loss experience when you feel like you've lost the will to continue on the low-carb plan for whatever reason. You'll feel like everything you've worked so hard to acheive has been for naught because you don't think you're losing weight fast enough or you just feel like you haven't been as successful as you had hoped. Believe me, you will have days like this and you need to know they are coming so you can be prepared to persevere through them.

Just as I became discouraged when I thought I had lost all that work I had invested in writing this book, you too will face temptation to quit your weight loss efforts even when you are doing quite well on your low-carb lifestyle. It is during these times that you need to stand firm in your belief that livin' la vida low-carb is the right way to go and that nothing will stand in the way of your meeting and even exceeding your goals. You need to press on to reach your goals.

You may need to reach out to those who have gone before you to offer you some assistance with helping you with your "corrupted" viewpoint and to remind you that what you are doing is having a positive impact on your health. Just as Christine retyped my book to restore it to where it was previously, it may take you a little extra work to get back on track with your low-carb plan. But the reward you will receive from doing this is immeasurable.

Persevering when times are tough is a good lesson in every part of our lives. Especially when you are trying to lose weight, it is important not to take your eye off of the ultimate prize of slimming down and regaining your health. Livin' la vida low-carb will help you get there and you should constantly remind yourself that what you are doing is working and will continue to work as long as you remain focused on the end result of all your hard work.

This might surprise you, but persevering is not as difficult as you might think. I'd like to share with you ten simple steps to remember that helped me persevere to reach my weight loss goals and still help me continue livin' la vida low-carb today.

1. **Plan to splurge one meal every 6-8 weeks.**

Shhhhhhh. Can you keep a secret? The strategic measure I am about to tell you is not in any previous book about low-carb, nor have I heard it recommended by anyone else who is livin' la vida low-carb. But it is something that helped keep me going especially during my weight loss phase and I even still use it today.

What is this amazing technique for persevering in your low-carb lifestyle? In a phrase, it's called a "planned splurge!"

Let's get one thing straight up front about what this is not. A "planned splurge" is not a mentality of "I'll cheat just this one time" or "I'll get off my low-carb lifestyle for this weekend" and promise to get back on it during the week. Additionally, it does not mean you get to eat whatever you want at any given moment as a spontaneous reaction to being placed in a situation where there is nothing low-carb for you to eat. That's not at all what I'm referring to.

My definition of a "planned splurge" is one that is scheduled way ahead of time on the calendar every six to eight weeks where you are allowed to eat whatever you want in the amount you want for one meal. Note that this is just for one meal, not a day or even a weekend, but one meal.

What does this do and how can it help you persevere through your weight loss?

First, it removes the temptation to get off your low-carb program in between your planned splurges because you will always have one upcoming on the calendar to look forward to. This was an incredibly effective plan for staying focused on my low-carb program because I knew I could eat whatever I wanted for one meal in just a few short weeks.

Second, you don't feel like you are depriving yourself of any food because you can always have it on your "planned splurge" meal if you really want it. Whether it's pizza, Mexican food, fast food or whatever, you'll always have a special surprise to look forward to every six to eight weeks.

Third, the "planned splurge" helps you celebrate the success you have already had and gives you an incentive to continue on with your weight loss plan. While this will most likely kick you out of ketosis for a few days, I found that I was able to get back on my low-carb plan very easily and return to my pre-"splurge" weight within just a few days. This was so helpful to me during the early stages of livin' la vida low-carb.

Remember, this is only valid for one meal and no more than that! I still use this "planned splurge" method today and have increased the frequency just slightly since I am no longer losing weight at the rapid pace I once did. It's incredibly effective and will help you persevere to meet your weight loss goals, too!

2. **Refuse to give up on your low-carb lifestyle no matter what.**

It should go without saying, but your decision to begin a low-carb lifestyle means you have made a conscious choice in your mind that you will never go back to the way you used to eat ever again. This is not a sad realization but rather a joyous one as you turn away from all those years of mindlessly eating anything and everything to satisfy your hungry appetite. Even still, your old habits will be hard to break so you must refuse to give up on your low-carb lifestyle no matter what.

It is unfortunate, but too often people get so down on themselves because they think they either messed up or aren't doing as well as they believe they should on their low-carb program. This often leads people to quit their weight loss plan despite the fact that they are at the brink of attaining great success. Changing this mentality will help you persevere and reach your goals and all the glory that comes with it. It can really happen if you stay focused on the task at hand.

Even when you hit the proverbial wall when there may be no weight loss at all, you have to keep moving forward with your low-carb plan as if you are still doing well. Ironically, you probably are succeeding at it even when the scale seems to be telling you otherwise.

I have said it before and I'll say it again, don't let that scale dictate your attitude about your weight loss. It is merely one way to measure how well you are doing. If it is discouraging you in your weight loss, then put it away for a while. You really won't need it when you are livin' la vida low-carb because you will lose inches on your body and start to feel better physically without having to know how much you weigh.

Part of refusing to give up means convincing yourself that nothing is going to derail you or sidetrack you as you pursue your weight loss. If there are doughnuts in the break room at work, then you know you can't have even one. The temporary pleasure from eating even just one of these carb-loaded, sugar-laced diet killers is not worth destroying everything you have worked so hard for on your low-carb plan. You are much better off to be prepared with your own low-carb snacks to keep you on track for the success you deserve.

3. **Think often about the people cheering you on to success as well as those who are expecting you to fail.**

Thinking about other reasons why I persevered in my weight loss, I can't help but recollect about all those people who were watching me. Many people were silently cheering me on to finally do something about my weight that will last. They eventually started verbalizing their praise once they started seeing results. But there were others who had seen me lose weight and gain it back before. Whether they would admit it or not, I am sure these people expected me to fail again. I just had to prove them wrong this time around.

When people try to discourage you in your weight loss, whether intentionally or not, it's important to remember those of us who have already been through the struggles and have overcome them triumphantly. The are countless millions of us low-carbers who are behind you 100 percent as you push towards the victory that is waiting for you at the finish line. We are standing there right now waiting for you to cross victorious over your weight problem.

Remember, this race is not about how fast you can sprint, but rather the endurance you will need to continue on to the very end. Keep your head down and trudge forward with all of your might. The payoff in the end will be so worth it!

4. Look in the mirror and ask yourself if the way you look now is the way you want to look for the rest of your life.

We all reach a point in our weight loss when we feel like our efforts are in vain and that we are investing a lot more in it than what it's worth. That is a very difficult mental hurdle to leap over, but is one that must be faced if you are going to be successful in your weight loss efforts.

Here's something quick and easy that you can do when you get to feeling this way.

Go to the closest mirror you can find. Make sure it is big enough for you to see your body from at least your waist up. Look at yourself intently and ask yourself, "Is this the way you want to look for the rest of your life?" I am not referring to your actual physical characteristics as much as I am your confidence in the way you see yourself. Our physical appearance can prevent us from feeling as good as we would like to, doesn't it? Let that motivate you to change and help you persevere while livin' la vida low-carb so you can make that change happen.

Remind yourself often that you can and will reach your weight loss goals so that you will some day look in that mirror and see that beautiful man or woman you already are. Visualizing what you will look like after losing weight can help you persevere to the end. Someday that vision will become a reality as your reflection will look back at you smiling proudly that you did something about your weight problem before it was too late.

5. Enjoy what you can eat and don't obsess about what you can't.

When people are on a diet and are not allowed to eat anything and everything in sight, it can be a little depressing. But, so is being overweight and feeling like there is nothing you can do about it. Most diets may make you start dwelling on all those foods you are not allowed to have anymore. I think this is the wrong kind of thinking, especially when you are livin' la vida low-carb.

Instead, what you should be focusing on are all the wonderful and delicious foods that you CAN have so you can make the most of your weight loss. When you are on a low-carb lifestyle, you have the luxury of enjoying great-tasting foods that will satisfy you and make you feel like you are eating normal. This way of eating makes it so easy to stick with and persevere because it tastes so good.

Food is not something that will control you any longer. You will be the one in the driver's seat about what you eat from now on and nothing is going to stand in your way of becoming that thin man or woman you have always wanted to be. Livin' la vida low-carb will help you get there.

6. Focus on how much better your health and life will be when you get down to the weight you need to be.

It's no secret that being overweight or obese is unhealthy. Most of us have heard that our entire lives from our doctor, our family and our friends. If you ever wanted good reasons to do something about your weight problem, then improved health and a better quality of life are good enough for me.

I had no idea what I was missing out on all these years of being overweight. For the first time in my life, I feel so much healthier and alive than ever thought possible. It's an amazing feeling to know you have done something positive about your health when you lose a lot of weight.

Just knowing that you will be adding many years back to your life by losing weight should help you persevere to the end of your weight loss goals. It certainly has for me and continues to give me a reason to keep the weight off forever.

7. If you happen to mess up, then it's not the end of the world.

One of the biggest reasons why people give up on their diets is because they mess up and think there is no way they can get back on their weight loss program. This is very similar to the misconception people have about God's love for them.

It is a sad fact, but most people think they have done too many things wrong for God to love them and accept them for who they are. They don't believe He will forgive them of their sins and restore their faith. But nothing could be further from the truth. Regardless of how much you disappoint God, He will still love you just the same because his love is unconditional. If you mess up, God will still be there to comfort you and help you get back on your feet.

The same goes for your weight loss efforts. If you decide to give in to temptation and have a slice of that chocolate cake at work, then it is not the end of the world. This is not a good excuse for getting off your weight loss program just because you made one little mistake. Instead, let this experience serve as a lesson about what not to do and get back on your plan immediately.

Persevering is not about being perfect in every aspect of your low-carb lifestyle. Everybody is going to react differently to their own individual program. The thing to remember is to pick yourself right back up and get it going again rather than beating yourself up over this. All that progress you have made will not suddenly disappear all at once. That should motivate you to keeping on to the end. You'll be glad that you did.

8. Don't micromanage your low-carb plan so much that you get frustrated by it.

Some people get so obsessive about their low-carb lifestyle that they feel they have to do it exactly down to every last detail or else they won't be successful. This is a very sad state to be in when you are trying to lose weight by livin' la vida low-carb because it can rob you of the joy you can have when you are finally free of the dieting rules.

There are a few people who try to do their own version of low-carb by severely restricting their carb intake to virtually zero carbs because they think that will help them reach their weight loss goals faster. This is unfortunate. The fact of the matter is the amount of carbs you can eat in a day will vary from person to person.

If you are one of those people who has to follow a program strictly with no variations whatsoever, then I encourage you to loosen up from that rigidity and enjoy your low-carb lifestyle. Micromanaging every little detail of this program will cause you to become discouraged and give up. It's hard to persevere when you have to work that hard at losing weight. The easy solution to this is don't do it!

9. Change your mental image of yourself from being fat to being skinny.

I can tell you now that I struggled with this point a lot during my yearlong weight loss. While I knew I was losing weight and my body was changing, the mental aspect of the weight loss was slow to sink in. Although my body was getting thinner and people were starting to call me "skinny" and "thin man," I still considered myself fat.

This is a mental thing that is very hard to shake, especially when you have been overweight for your entire life. It took me a while, but I eventually came to the realization that I wasn't that 410-pound man I used to be and I was now weighing in at a healthy and thin 230 pounds. Changing this mental image of yourself will make persevering in your low-carb lifestyle that much easier.

10. **Make this low-carb lifestyle change permanent.**

Since this is the subject of the final chapter of this book, I will expand upon this point completely in the upcoming pages.

KEY POINTS TO REMEMBER FROM CHAPTER 9:

- When you are tempted or discouraged, just press on

- Plan a splurge meal every 6-8 weeks

- Don't give up on your low-carb lifestyle no matter what

- Think about the people who are watching you

- Be happy with the way you look or change it if you aren't

- Enjoy what you can eat and don't obsess about what you can't

- Realize you are improving your health and quality of life

- If you mess up, don't let it discourage you

- Don't feel like you have to be perfect on your low-carb program

- Change your mental self-image to the thin person you are becoming

Chapter 10
Stay Committed For Life

Now that I've lost 180 pounds and kept it off for a little while, I still often get asked the question, "Are you still on your diet?" I usually grin back at the person who asked the question and retort, "Do you mean, am I still eating low-carb?" After their blank look of confusion subsides, I explain that while I am no longer losing weight as rapidly as I once did on my new way of eating, I am still on a low-carb lifestyle to keep the weight off permanently.

I have committed myself to eating this way for the rest of my life. As the song says, you need to dance with the one that brung ya! That's why I have confidently said throughout this book that I am livin' la vida low-carb. The changes in my way of thinking about healthy eating, exercise and nutrition have helped me reach this point where I will stay committed to low-carb for life. If not, then I know that I'll be on a one-way ticket right back to being overweight again and probably worse. I'm bound and determined that will never ever happen to me again!

Going on a "diet" just feels bad and that's why most of us low-carbers consider our way of eating to be a healthy lifestyle change rather than the dreaded "d"-word. If you have the mentality "getting off" your diet once the weight is gone, then nothing in the world is going to work for you to keep your weight off forever. Until you realize that the eating habits you have when you are overweight or obese are what caused you to get that way in the first place, then you will never make the transition to the kind of eating habits you will need to enjoy a long and healthy life. My friend Adam Wilk wrote a humorous, yet refreshingly honest book about dieting in his pseudo-autobiographical book called <u>Diet King</u>. Check it out!

That's why livin' la vida low-carb is the one and only eating plan you will ever need to follow even after losing your weight. But even if you happen to choose to follow a low-fat diet, then that should be your one and only diet for the rest of your entire life (gee, that's a scary thought, isn't it?!). The point is to find whatever it is that works for you and then stick with it. This isn't rocket science people!

It is important to remember that while I found tremendous success on the low-carb lifestyle, not everyone is going to necessarily have the same results. Your low-carb program may need to be tailored to meet your individual needs in a different way than mine. Make sure you personalize your own plan to cater to who you are and don't simply try to replicate what I did word for word. That'll serve you well as you go about implementing a low-carb strategy in your own life.

Life has been different in so many ways since I lost weight on low-carb that I cannot even begin to count the ways. I'm breathing better, I'm feeling better, and nothing can diminish the newfound confidence I have to tell the whole world what this way of eating has done for me. I honestly believe that many more people could benefit greatly from a low-carb lifestyle change and I am enthusiastically telling everyone I know about how this experience has turned my life upside down for the better.

I hope my story of struggle, hope and triumph has encouraged you to make this your lifestyle change and motivated you to stay committed for life. It took me a very long time to figure out what needed to be done to lose weight for good. But now that I've found a way that worked for me, I can't help but share this amazing weight loss method with anyone who will listen.

While I really do not believe I have achieved anything until I can keep the weight off for at least three years (that would be January 1, 2008), I believe I have made the necessary changes in my habits to confidently say this lifestyle change has taken hold in my life. If you are going to be successful in your low-carb program, then making this your permanent way of eating is essential to making that happen.

Eating low-carb has become such a way of life for so many people, myself included, that it is not going anywhere anytime soon despite negative reports you may read about in the meida. When I committed myself to eating low-carb as a permanent lifestyle change on January 1, 2004, it was not a half-hearted change. I am a lifetime low-carb eater from now until the day I die because I am living proof of its life-changing effect.

Dr. Robert Atkins wrote a book entitled <u>Atkins For Life</u> that deals with this subject of what to do once you've reached your weight loss goals. It has additional information that will help you stay committed for life as you are livin' la vida low-carb. It is an excellent resource for anyone who wants to know what to do next after the weight loss phase of low-carb has concluded.

Life after my enormous weight loss has certainly been exciting, but also a little bit disappointing. As a result of losing as much weight as quickly as I did, I now have a lot of loose, hanging skin, especially in my stomach. As you can imagine, going from a size 62 to a 40-inch waist was no small feat and my body just could not take up the slack. I know it's gross to talk about hanging skin, but reality is reality. I'm thankful the weight is gone now, but what is left is simply unsightly to look at. It's also in a few other areas of my body, but the biggest problem is right there in the belly!

My health insurance company has been totally unresponsive to letters from my doctor confirming my enormous weight loss. They consider the abdominoplasty, or tummy tuck, to be a purely cosmetic procedure and medically unnecessary. Never mind the fact that I've lost 180 pounds, exercise every day, helped my cardiovascular health, lowered my cholesterol, decreased my blood pressure and greatly improved my overall health for the long-term, they don't want to pay for something that is (in their minds) not a health issue.

Well, what am I supposed to do with what is ostensibly 10-15 pounds of dead skin that has lost its elasticity in an area of my body that will not improve on its own? I do about 100 ab crunches as part of my weight lifting routine. I would like to eventually be able to see those abdominal muscles that I am building up underneath that skin and to be able to walk around without a shirt on so I can truly feel skinny for the first time in my life. As long as that skin remains, that will not happen!

I sent my weight loss success story to several popular television talk shows hoping that one of them would call me and ask me to be on their show. While I don't expect that call will ever come, I am still hopeful that it may yet still happen so I can get the surgery done that needs to be done.

I just don't have $12,000 that I can plop down at the drop of a button as well as two months out of work. It's a dream for me to have this done, but I can dream, can't I? If this book is a huge success, then maybe I will be able to fund my weight loss surgery that way. Again, I'll hope for the best because this procedure will need to be done at some point in the near future. Oprah, Maury, are you listening?

As for my weight since I stopped losing, it has remained fairly constant ever since. While it may go up a couple of pounds one day and down a couple the next, for the most part I have been within 5-10 pounds of my lowest weight of 230 since I stopped losing at the beginning of 2005.

I believe the weight lifting has caused me to gain some muscle while I have still continued to lose fat. I also started taking Creatine to help with my weight lifting and my personal trainer said that will cause most people to gain about 10-20 pounds. Since my weight has not gone up that dramatically, I assume I have lost more weight there. If my weight begins to drop down below 230, that'll be fine, too. I figure my body will stop losing when I have no more weight to lose.

And, in case you are wondering, I have added back a lot more carbohydrates than what I ate during my weight loss phase. In fact, with the weight lifting training, I have found that I am a lot more hungry and can get away with eating more food than I did before. Now that's a nice bonus!

In the meantime, I'm eating about 75-100 carbohydrates of delicious foods per day combined with my cardio and weight training. It is a lifestyle I have committed myself to 100%! People ask me how I made the switch from a fat slob into an athletic overachiever. I tell them it was easy once I realized it wasn't as hard as I thought it was going to be and just did it.

It's not about willpower, or determination, or even self-discipline. While all of those things are important, I tell people just to have fun and find something that works for them. That's what will make you a success at losing weight or winning at life. God will place the desire in your heart to be who you were meant to be. It is your choice about whether you will follow through to make it a reality.

If you take nothing else from this book except the knowledge that one man was able to overcome a lifetime of disappointments trying to lose weight, then this book will have been worth all those months of writing that I invested in it. The principles that helped me can certainly help get you started right on your own journey from flabby fat to sensationally skinny. I can't promise you will replicate my success, but I can promise you this will be the most fun you'll ever have on a diet.

Now get out there and start livin' la vida low-carb!

Livin' With The Low-Carb Man
by Christine Moore

When Jimmy mentioned he wanted to lose weight on the low-carb lifestyle, I have to admit I was skeptical, but excited about the prospect. He had tried so many diets before and had failed on all of them in the past.

In fact, he promised me before we got married in 1995 that he would lose weight before the wedding. But obviously that didn't happen and he's been progressively gaining weight ever since.

That is, until he started this low-carb thing in 2004.

When Jimmy started low-carb, I could see a newfound excitement and determination in him that showed me he might actually pull this off this time around. I was thrilled when I noticed my husband's weight was coming off so quickly.

One of the things that I had to get used to was the new eating habits Jimmy had implemented to do his low-carb lifestyle. I had to learn how to cater the meals to fit his low-carb way of eating and that was a real challenge in the beginning. But, eventually, I got the hang of it.

In February 2004, Jimmy came to me and mentioned that he was going to start exercising. My jaw literally hit the floor because if you knew Jimmy, this bit of news would come as a shock to you. But to my surprise, he actually started a regular exercise routine and stuck with it.

In fact, in April 2005 after he had lost 180 pounds, I saw my husband do something that I had never ever seen him do in the ten years we have been married. He actually did an all-out sprint to our car wearing a suit and dress shoes from about a quarter mile away and he didn't even lose his breath. Now that was amazing!

As I saw Jimmy's weight loss slow down after a few months on his low-carb plan, I thought it was important to encourage him to keep going because I didn't want him to fail again. Much to my delight, Jimmy stayed strong even when things got really tough. I knew just a gentle word from me here and there would keep him strong through the slow periods of his weight loss.

Now that he has committed himself to this low-carb lifestyle, I am more at ease about his overall health than I have been since we got married. I have to admit that this has been a genuine prayer concern of mine for many, many years and it is incomprehensible that Jimmy has finally overcome his weight problem.

I want to conclude by saying that I am so very proud of Jimmy and that I wish him the very best in keeping the weight off for good with low-carb. That's what life is like livin' with the low-carb man.

I love you, honey!

Hugs and kisses,

Christine

WOODBRIDGE TOWN LIBRARY
10 NEWTON ROAD
WOODBRIDGE, CT 06525

Printed in the United States
54609LVS00003B/371

9 781591 138044